Penguin
Random
House

Senior designers Michelle Staples, Jacqui Swan
Lead editor Amanda Wyatt
Editors Steven Carton, Ben Morgan
US editor Kayla Dugger
Designers Sean T. Ross, Chrissy Barnard, Alex Lloyd,
Gregory McCarthy, Mary Sandberg
Illustrators Alex Lloyd, Sean T. Ross, Gus Scott

Managing editor Lisa Gillespie
Managing art editor Owen Peyton Jones
Producer, pre-production Gill Reid
Senior producer Meskerem Berhane
Jacket designers Tanya Mehrotra, Surabhi Wadhwa-Gandhi
Design development manager Sophia MTT
Jackets editor Emma Dawson
Managing jackets editor Saloni Singh
Jackets editorial coordinator Priyanka Sharma
Jacket DTP designer Rakesh Kumar
Picture researcher Rituraj Singh

Publisher Andrew Macintyre
Associate publishing director Liz Wheeler
Art director Karen Self
Publishing director Jonathan Metcalf

Writer and consultant Jack Challoner
Photographer Dave King

Smithsonian

SMITHSONIAN

Established in 1846, the Smithsonian—the world's largest museum and research complex—includes 19 museums and galleries and the National Zoological Park. The total number of artifacts, works of art, and specimens in the Smithsonian's collection is estimated at 154 million. The Smithsonian is a renowned research center, dedicated to public education, national service, and scholarship in the arts, sciences, and history.

First American Edition, 2019
Published in the United States by DK Publishing
345 Hudson Street, New York, New York 10014

Copyright © 2019 Dorling Kindersley Limited
DK, a Division of Penguin Random House LLC
19 20 21 22 23 10 9 8 7 6 5 4 3 2 1
001-310899-Jan/2019

A catalog record for this book
is available from the Library of Congress.
ISBN: 978-1-4654-7561-9

DK books are available at special discounts when purchased in bulk for sales promotions, premiums, fund-raising, or educational use. For details, contact:
DK Publishing Special Markets, 345 Hudson Street, New York, New York 10014
SpecialSales@dk.com

Printed and bound in China

A WORLD OF IDEAS:
SEE ALL THERE IS TO KNOW

www.dk.com

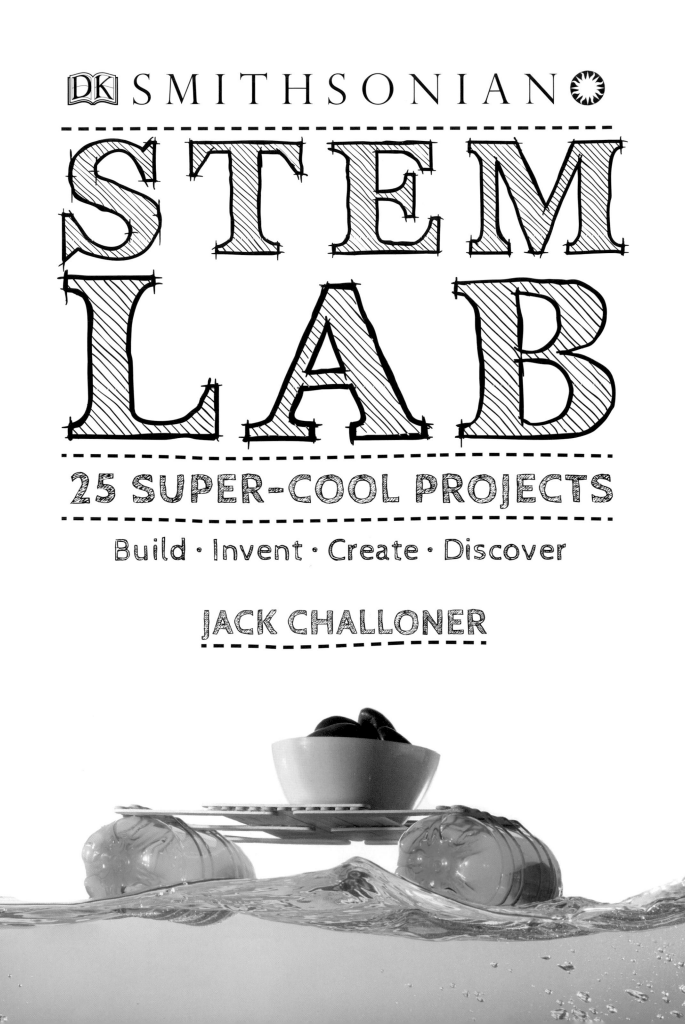

DK · SMITHSONIAN

STEM LAB

25 SUPER-COOL PROJECTS

Build · Invent · Create · Discover

JACK CHALLONER

CONTENTS

SCIENCE FACTS
This symbol points out facts about biology, chemistry, or physics.

TECHNOLOGY FACTS
This symbol highlights more information about tools or materials.

ENGINEERING FACTS
This symbol directs you to more facts about structures or machines.

MATHEMATICS FACTS
This symbol identifies extra information on formulas, shapes, or measurements.

FOREWORD

Welcome to STEM Lab—a book full of exciting activities for you to do, mostly with things you can find around your home or get ahold of easily.

The "Lab" part of the book's title comes from two previous books I have written: "Maker Lab" and "Maker Lab: Outdoors." If you haven't seen them, why not check them out? They have some great projects, too.

The "STEM" part of the book's title stands for "Science, Technology, Engineering, and Mathematics." Throughout this book, I have used these words when explaining how the activities work or describing how they relate to everyday life. I want to tell you a bit about what these things are, and what they mean to me.

Science is the process of finding out about the world around us—through observing, thinking, and experimenting. For people like me who are curious about what stuff is made of and how things work, science is fascinating. In this book, you'll find projects exploring chemical reactions, discover how waves behave, and learn about the science of sound.

Technology is all about the devices and tools that make our lives better or easier. Screwdrivers, microwaves, toilets, and airplanes are all examples of the enormous variety of technologies that surround us. With the help of this book, I hope you'll enjoy discovering how some key technologies work—from a wind turbine to a tower crane. It's exciting to imagine what sort of inventions might be developed by future minds!

Engineering explores the materials from which things are made and the techniques used to make them. Engineers design, test, and make buildings, cars, bridges, and tunnels, for example. If you like making things and choosing the right material and method for a task, then you'll love engineering. This book includes activities that illustrate some important principles of engineering—you'll learn how to build an almost-indestructible sandcastle and a super-strong dome from paper straws.

Mathematics is the world of numbers and shapes. It is an essential part of science, technology, and engineering, but it is a joy in itself. In numbers and shapes, there is beauty that everyone can enjoy. You'll find mathematics in nearly all the activities, whether it be measurements and angles or the precision needed to make a project work well.

These four subject areas are interrelated, and by combining them, new insights, ideas, skills, and solutions to problems emerge. Furthermore, some people add an "A" to STEM, turning it into STEAM. The "A" stands for Art. I like that, because it reminds us that STEM is creative, and that science, technology, engineering, art, and mathematics are all important ways to understand the world around us, so that we can hopefully make it a better place.

Remember to take care with some of the activities and watch out for any warnings accompanying an activity. Be sure to ask an adult if you need help with a tricky step.

JACK CHALLONER

FORCES AND MOTION

A force is a push or a pull, and there are forces at work everywhere! Forces can make things move or stop moving, make things speed up or slow down, or just keep things still. One of the most familiar forces is gravity, which pulls everything down toward the ground. In this chapter, you'll be fighting against gravity by constructing a crane and by making a ping-pong ball hover in the air. You'll also explore the forces that make a raft stay afloat.

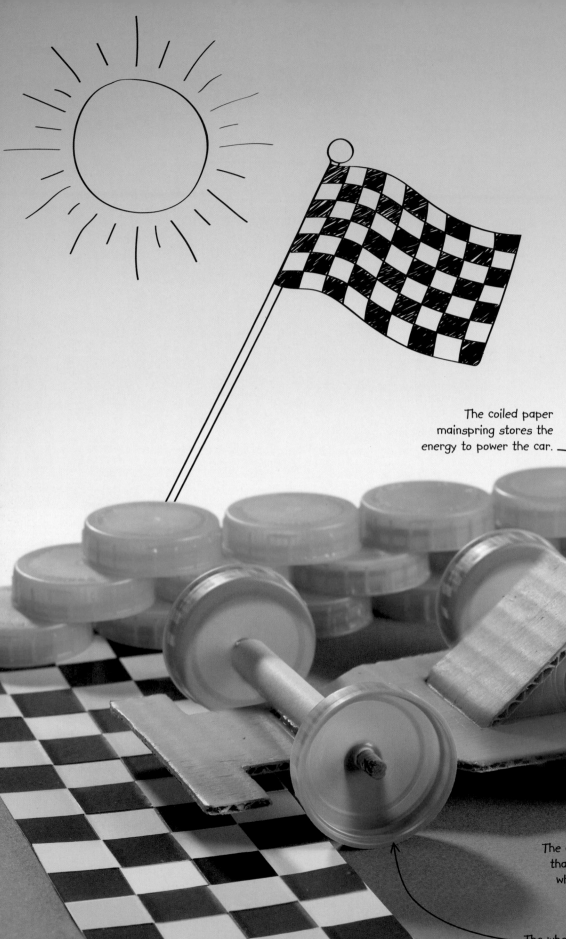

The coiled paper mainspring stores the energy to power the car.

The axle is the rod that connects the wheels together.

The wheels are made of plastic bottle caps.

POTENTIAL ENERGY
WIND-UP CAR

Used for centuries to make clocks and moving toys, wind-up mechanisms have long, coiled strips of springy material called mainsprings that store energy as they're tightened. Energy can't be created or destroyed—it can only be transferred. So as you wind up the car, its mainspring stores the energy you put into turning it. Let it go, and VROOM! The energy is released, and your car is off!

The more you tighten the mainspring, the more energy is stored in it.

The car has three bearings—narrow tubes made from paper that allow the axles to turn freely.

When two surfaces rub together, a force known as friction is produced. Friction acts at the car's axle as it turns in the bearing and where the wheels meet the ground.

HOW TO MAKE A
WIND-UP CAR

This wind-up car is powered by energy stored in a coiled mainspring made of paper. Its axles (the rods connecting the wheels) are made from a garden stake, while its bearings (the tubes that allow the axles to turn freely) are made with paper. The axles and bearings are attached to the car's frame, or chassis.

Time
30 minutes

Difficulty
Medium

WHAT YOU NEED

Double-sided tape

Four bottle caps

Paint

Pencil

Glue

Garden stake

Paintbrush

Scissors

Adhesive putty

8½x11 piece of paper

Cardboard

Ruler

1 Draw a rectangle 6 in (15 cm) long and 3 in (8 cm) wide on the cardboard. Use a ruler to make sure your lines are straight. With the scissors, carefully cut out the rectangle you drew.

This piece will be the chassis, the main frame of the car.

2 At one end of your chassis, draw two dots, each ¾ in (2 cm) in from the end and from the side. Draw a line that passes through the dots.

2 in (5 cm)

Vertical line

Make sure when you draw the two lines that they are parallel to each other.

3 Draw two lines 2 in (5 cm) long at right angles from the vertical line you just drew, each one starting at one of the dots.

Ask an adult to help you if you find this step difficult.

4 Using scissors, carefully cut along the middle of the vertical line, then down the two lines you just drew, to create a flap.

This line should be ½ in (1 cm) from the edge.

2¾ in (7 cm)

5 Draw two more lines parallel to the first one, about ½ in (1 cm) and 2¾ in (7 cm) from the other end of your chassis.

The dots should be ¾ in (2 cm) in from each end of this line.

6 Make dots ¾ in (2 cm) in from each end of the line nearest the end, and draw a smooth curve from the dots to the ends of the other line. Cut along the curves.

7 Paint the chassis. We've used green paint, but you can choose whatever color you like.

8 On a piece of paper, draw two lines, 1¼ in (3 cm) and 2½ in (6 cm) in, from one of the long sides of the paper.

Paper is a thin, versatile material made from mashed-up wood fibers.

9 Cut along the two lines to make two long strips. These will be used to make the mainspring.

10 Use a small strip of double-sided tape to join the two pieces of paper together into one long piece.

The double-sided tape will allow you to seal the paper's top edge onto the tube.

Don't roll the paper too tightly, as your car's axle will need to turn inside it.

11 Take the rest of the sheet of paper and roll it lengthwise around the garden stake to make a tube. Secure the tube with double-sided tape.

12 Draw lines on the tube at distances of ¾, 1½, and 5 in (2, 4, and 12 cm) from one end. These pieces will be your bearings.

Paper becomes very strong when it is rolled up.

13 Cut the tube along the lines you drew. You should end up with two pieces ½ in (1 cm) long and one piece 1½ in (4 cm) long. You don't need the rest of the paper tube, so try to recycle it.

14 Carefully cut two 4½ in (11 cm) lengths of garden stake. If you have trouble cutting it safely or neatly, ask an adult to help. These will be your axles.

15 Tape one end of your long strip of paper to the middle of one of your garden stake axles. Coil the paper around the axle.

Once it is wound up, the car's mainspring will store potential energy.

Put the tape here.

16 Turn the chassis upside down and push the coiled mainspring through the flap of cardboard. Use double-sided tape to secure it.

Put one short paper tube onto this end of the axle.

Slide the second short tube onto this end of the axle.

17 Turn the chassis over again and slip one short paper tube over each end of the axle. Glue them in place.

18 Slip the longer paper tube over the other garden stake axle and glue that in place near the other end of the chassis.

Leave the glue to dry completely so it's really strong.

Be sure to protect the table and your fingers with adhesive putty.

19 Use the pencil to make a small hole in the center of each of the four bottle caps. Use adhesive putty to protect the table and your fingers.

Make sure the axles are parallel to the ends of the chassis.

20 Push the bottle caps over the ends of the axle to give your car wheels. If they are loose, secure them with adhesive putty or glue.

Energy can't be created or destroyed. It can only be transferred.

21 To make your car go, you have to wind up the mainspring. Do this by placing the car on the ground and pulling it backward. Let go and watch it speed off!

You can work out your car's average speed by dividing the distance it travels by how long it takes.

The mainspring's energy is converted into kinetic energy, then lost as heat at the axles and ground due to friction and air resistance.

HOW IT WORKS

Your car demonstrates potential and kinetic energy. Potential energy is stored energy, ready to make things happen. Kinetic energy is the energy objects have when they move. When you wind up the mainspring, you are storing potential energy, which will be used to make the car travel forward. The faster an object moves and the more mass it has, the more kinetic energy it has. You can calculate the amount of energy a moving object has: multiply its mass (the amount of matter, or stuff it is made of) by its speed squared, then divide by 2.

The mainspring is coiled up tightly.

1 As you pull the car backward, the turning wheels coil the mainspring tightly, storing energy. When you let go, the spring uncoils and the potential energy becomes kinetic energy. The car moves forward.

TEST AND TWEAK

Your wind-up car should zoom across the floor or table as the mainspring unwinds. Test it out on different surfaces and adapt its design to see if you can make your car go farther and faster.

SANDPAPER WHEELS

Try wrapping sandpaper around the rear wheels to increase the amount of friction between them and the ground.

RUBBER BANDS

Putting rubber bands around the wheels gives the wheels extra traction, or grip, like the rubber tires of a real car.

CARD MAINSPRING

A mainspring made of cardstock should make your car go faster, as cardstock stores more energy than paper. But it will release this energy faster, so your car won't travel as far.

REAL WORLD: TECHNOLOGY
ELECTRIC CARS

Most cars use the chemical potential energy stored in gasoline to move, but not all. Electric cars have powerful batteries that store electrical potential energy. They can be recharged, like a smartphone.

REAL WORLD: MATH
AIR RESISTANCE

Moving cars encounter a force called air resistance, which slows them down. Air resistance increases with speed. If you double the speed of the moving vehicle, the air resistance quadruples.

2 The spring continues uncoiling and the car keeps moving. Its kinetic energy is lost as heat. This happens through friction (at the axles and the ground) and air resistance.

The mainspring has completely uncoiled and can provide no more energy for the car.

3 You can't feel the heat generated by friction and air resistance, as there isn't much kinetic energy in the first place. Once the kinetic energy is lost, the car stops.

BOTTLE RAFT

This activity could save your life! If you were stranded on a desert island and you had some large empty barrels, you could make a raft to escape! It's a simple matter of balancing forces. The bowl of pebbles on the lollipop stick platform pushes the raft downward into the water, but this force is balanced out by the buoyancy, or "upthrust," of the water pressing against the air-filled plastic bottles. Because these forces are equal, the raft floats!

The raft's platform is made of lollipop sticks, which are strong but light.

The bottles are filled with air, which makes them lighter than water.

This bowl of pebbles is acting as a load—a force that the raft's structure can withstand.

When the raft is placed in water, the water pushes upward on the bottles with a force called buoyancy, or "upthrust."

HOW TO BUILD A
BOTTLE RAFT

Empty plastic bottles float well in water, but to make an effective raft, you need to build a platform on which to support the load. It's a fairly simple project—the raft's platform is made of lollipop sticks glued together, and it is attached to the bottles with stretched rubber bands.

Time
30 minutes

Difficulty
Medium

WHAT YOU NEED

Bowl of pebbles

Rubber bands

Glue

23 lollipop sticks

Scales

Two 16 oz (500 ml) bottles

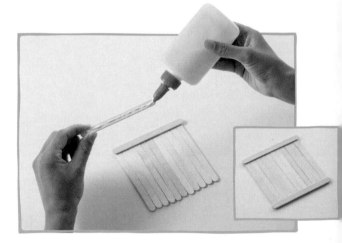

1 Lay 11 lollipop sticks side by side. Secure them together by adding glue to two other lollipop sticks and positioning them on either side of the platform.

2 Take three lollipop sticks. Space them evenly so that they stretch the length of one lollipop stick. Put glue at the far end of each stick.

Rubber is an elastic (stretchy) material, so it can fit around your bottles.

3 Press two lollipop sticks on top of the dabs of glue to make an E-shape. Repeat steps 2 and 3 to make a second E-shape.

4 Once the glue on your two E-shapes has dried, slip two rubber bands over the ends of each one.

Before sticking the E-shapes to your platform, check that you have four rubber bands on each E-shape.

5 After you've placed the rubber bands onto both your E-shapes, turn the raft's platform over and glue the E-shapes onto it at both ends. Use lots of glue. Leave it to dry completely.

6 Stretch the rubber bands one by one enough to push the bottles through. Try to ensure that the rubber bands are evenly spaced.

Rafts are usually built with light materials, such as wood, plastic, or foam.

The caps keep your raft airtight and watertight.

8 Float your raft in the sink or bathtub, or even on a pond. (Make sure you have an adult with you.) Gently place the bowl of pebbles on top of your raft's platform ... can it take the load?

7 Use scales to weigh the bowl and the pebbles, so you can see how heavy a load your raft is able to carry.

The strength of the join between the frame and platform might limit how heavy a load your raft can take. How can you make it stronger?

What would happen if the bottles were filled with water instead of air?

TEST AND TWEAK

See how much weight your raft can support by experimenting with heavier loads. You could also adapt your raft to make a bridge or even a boat. To make a boat, add a sail to give it propulsion and a rudder underneath to help it steer a straight path.

This large bowl of sand is heavier than the bowl of pebbles. What happens if you put it on your raft?

To support heavier loads, you could use bigger bottles or more bottles to make the raft more buoyant.

A pontoon is a bridge made by tying boats together. To turn your raft into a pontoon, simply add more platforms and bottles!

HOW IT WORKS

Whether or not an object floats depends on something called density. Density is how much mass (stuff) an object contains relative to its volume (the amount of space it takes up). When you place an object in water, the water pushes it upward with a force called buoyancy. If an object is more dense than water, the buoyancy is too weak to support its weight, and the object sinks. That's why small, heavy things like coins and stones sink. Objects with low density, like your air-filled plastic bottles, are less dense than water, so the buoyancy supports their weight and makes them float. Any object more dense than water will sink, and any object less dense will float.

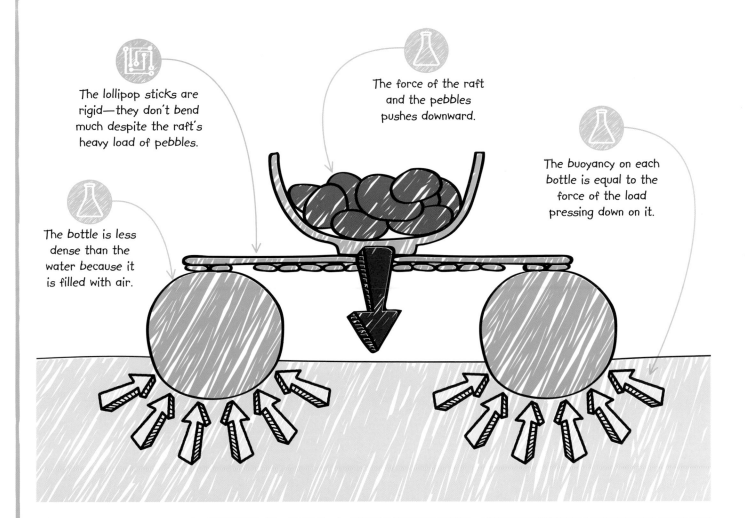

The lollipop sticks are rigid—they don't bend much despite the raft's heavy load of pebbles.

The force of the raft and the pebbles pushes downward.

The buoyancy on each bottle is equal to the force of the load pressing down on it.

The bottle is less dense than the water because it is filled with air.

REAL WORLD: ENGINEERING
SUBMARINES

Submarines can change their buoyancy—that's how they rise to the surface and dive deep. They have tanks that can be filled with water or air. At the surface, they take water into those tanks, increasing their density—so they sink. To rise up, air is pumped into the tanks, reducing their density and allowing them to float up to the surface.

SAND PENDULUM

You can draw *beautiful* patterns with lines of sand by making a simple swinging device called a pendulum. All you need is some sand, a plastic bottle, and a long piece of string. This activity is a lot of fun to watch, but there's plenty of science to think about, too—like how the force of gravity makes the pendulum swing back and forth.

As the swinging
pendulum spirals
inward, it produces
beautiful patterns.

We've used brightly
colored sand, but you
could use ordinary
sand or salt.

HOW TO MAKE A
SAND PENDULUM

For this activity, you'll need plenty of space. We've used green-colored sand, but ordinary sand is fine, too. Make sure your sand is perfectly dry; otherwise, it won't flow freely. If you don't have sand, you can use salt instead.

Time
30 minutes

Difficulty
Medium

WHAT YOU NEED

String

Pencil

Scissors

Duct tape

Adhesive putty

Long ruler

Hole punch

Plastic bottle

Colored sand, plain sand, or salt

Large sheets of dark paper

Screw the cap back on with the adhesive putty in place.

1 Place the cap of the bottle upside down on a lump of adhesive putty. Use the scissors to make a hole about $\frac{1}{8}$ in (3 mm) wide in the middle.

Ask an adult if you find this part tricky.

2 Using the scissors, cut off the bottom of the bottle. Try to cut in a straight line.

The hole punch creates a neat round hole.

3 Use the hole punch to make three evenly spaced holes in the plastic bottle, about ½ in (1 cm) away from the edge that you cut.

4 Measure and cut a piece of string about 10 in (25 cm) long.

Make sure the knots are secure.

5 Tie the string to two of the holes in the bottle to make a loop.

6 Cut a second length of string at least 7 ft (2 m) long. Tie one end of it to the third hole in the bottle.

Adjust the position of this knot to make the bottle hang straight.

7 Tie the long piece of string to the loop, taking care to keep the three lengths of string from each hole equal in length. This will help your bottle hang straight.

String is made from woven plant fibers.

8 Ask an adult to help you suspend the pendulum from a high point (such as the branch of a tree or a hook on a ceiling) so the bottle cap is 2 in (4–5 cm) above the ground. Pour sand or salt into the bottle.

9 Use the duct tape to join a few sheets of the dark paper. This will make one large piece to catch the sand that falls from the bottle.

10 Remove the adhesive putty and give the bottle a gentle sideways push to make it swing in a circle. Once the bottle is empty, fold up the paper and tip the sand back into the bottle. You can then try the experiment again.

The pendulum slowly loses energy due to friction between the string and the point where it is tied, and air resistance between the bottle and the air.

The bottle moves in oval shapes called ellipses.

The ellipses get smaller as the pendulum loses energy.

TEST AND TWEAK

In the 1580s, the Italian scientist Galileo discovered that a pendulum swings back and forth in a straight line for a precise time, or period, that depends on its length—a discovery that eventually led to the invention of pendulum clocks. Try changing the length of your pendulum to see how it affects the time it takes to swing back and forth in a straight line. You can also make the pendulum's elliptical movements more complex by making the string Y-shaped. This gives the pendulum a short period in one direction and a long period in another, resulting in weird and wonderful sand patterns known as Lissajous curves. If you raise or lower the meeting point between the Y's arms, the Lissajous curves will change.

Changing the position of this knot results in different sand patterns.

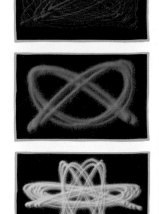

HOW IT WORKS

If you simply pulled your pendulum away from its resting point and let go, it would swing back and forth in a straight line until it ran out of energy. Because you pushed it sideways, it swung along a curving path—an ellipse—continually changing direction. A moving object only changes direction when a force acts on it. In this case, the force of gravity is pulling the bottle back to the middle, but its sideways motion and the pull of the string stop it from returning directly. The pendulum loses energy due to friction. As a result, it slowly spirals inward, the sand tracing out a beautiful record of its path.

Tension in the string pulls upward at an angle.

The result of the two forces shown here is a "net force" pulling the pendulum inward.

Gravity pulls downward.

FROM THE SIDE

The pendulum's initial sideways push prevents it from moving inward directly, so it moves in ellipses instead.

Inward force

Sand

FROM THE TOP

REAL WORLD: SCIENCE
ORBITING OBJECTS

The artificial satellites orbiting our planet travel in ellipses or circles, just like your sand pendulum. There is just one force acting on all these orbiting objects: gravity. It pulls the satellites inward, causing them to curve continually around Earth rather than flying off into space.

The blades will turn more easily if they're at a slight angle to the wind.

The shaft rotates as the blades move. This motion winds the string, which lifts the bucket.

The curved blades deflect the wind. This makes the blades move in the opposite direction.

WIND TURBINE

Have you ever seen huge wind turbines spinning slowly around? The blades are being pushed around by the energy of the wind. Inside each tower is an electrical generator, which converts wind energy into electrical energy to power homes, offices, factories, and schools. You can explore the engineering challenge of extracting energy from the wind by building your own wind turbine using paper cups to make the blades.

The bigger the blades, the greater the area through which they sweep and the more energy the turbine can capture.

HOW TO MAKE A

WIND TURBINE

Perhaps the most important feature of a wind turbine is the fact that the *blades are at an angle*, so they deflect the wind. This turbine's blades are made from paper cups, which are naturally curved, so they deflect the wind and work well. Take time to make your turbine, waiting for the glue to set where necessary.

Time
45 minutes

Difficulty
Medium

WHAT YOU NEED

Garden stake

Ruler

Paintbrush

Pencil

Paint

Adhesive putty

Scissors

String

Weight

Glue

Four lollipop sticks

Tall paper cup

Small paper cup

Three medium paper cups

1 Take two medium cups and draw a line on the side of one 2¾ in (7 cm) from the bottom. Draw a line 2 in (5 cm) from the *bottom* of the other cup.

2 With a pair of scissors, carefully cut around the lines and remove the top part of both cups. Discard the tops—recycle them, if possible.

3 Using the sharp point of the pencil, poke a hole at the center of the *base* of each medium cup. Take care not to poke yourself!

4 Insert the smaller of the two shortened cups into the larger one. Squeeze glue into the joint to fit them together and wait for the glue to dry.

The shorter cup is upside down.

5 Make a pencil mark 10 in (25 cm) from one end of the garden stake.

Use scissors to score the stick.

6 Cut the garden stake at the pencil mark. Score the stick with scissors first, then bend it to snap it. Ask an adult if you find this tricky.

 This stick performs the job of the shaft in a real wind turbine. The shaft helps convert wind energy into electricity.

7 Slide the stick through the holes in the bases of the two joined cups.

8 Place the tall, uncut cup upside down and glue a lollipop stick to either side of the base, making sure each one reaches the same distance above the cup.

9 Wait until the glue has dried, then spread glue on the inside surfaces of the two lollipop sticks, near the end.

10 Place the joined cups with the stick through the center between the lollipop sticks. Hold the cups in place while the glue dries.

11 To make the turbine blades, take your remaining medium-sized cup and carefully cut it in half down the side with a pair of scissors.

12 Cut each half in half again so you are left with four equal pieces. Cut the base of each quarter off and recycle these pieces.

Make sure the blades all face the same way.

13 Place glue at the center of a lollipop stick and stick it to another to form a cross. Glue the edges of your blades to the lollipop sticks.

On a real wind turbine, the blades are able to move on their axes to face wherever the wind is coming from.

14 Stick a piece of adhesive putty to the center of the cross. The adhesive putty will secure the blades to the shaft.

15 To attach the blades to the wind turbine, attach the adhesive putty to the end of the stick in the top of the turbine.

Hold some adhesive putty on the inside of the cup to avoid hurting yourself.

The string will act as the bucket's handle.

16 Take the small cup and make three equally spaced small holes around the top using a sharp pencil. This will be your load-lifting bucket.

17 To connect the bucket to the wind turbine, cut a 5 in (12 cm) piece of string. Thread the string through two of the holes in the bucket and tie a knot at either end to secure it in place.

The wind turbine's blades are curved, helping them to deflect the wind.

18 Measure and cut a 16 in (40 cm) piece of string. Thread one end of the string through the third hole in the bucket, then tie it to the middle of the short piece of string.

19 Tie the free end of the long string to the garden stake. If you want to be sure it won't slip, secure it with a small piece of tape.

 20 Now paint and decorate your wind turbine in your favorite colors and patterns.

The curved blades of this wind turbine transfer some of the kinetic (movement) energy in the wind into rotary (turning) motion in the blades.

If the wind turbine falls over when it's carrying a load, stick some modeling clay inside the base to act as a weight.

21 Now you can try it out! Put weights in the bucket and see how quickly it rises when you expose the turbine to wind. If there's no wind, you could use a fan or a hairdryer. What happens to the bucket when the wind stops? Does it fall back down, or does friction hold it in place?

Put different weights in the bucket to see how much your wind turbine can lift.

TEST AND TWEAK

If you have a fan with different speed settings, investigate how quickly the windmill lifts the bucket as the wind speed increases. Try making different kinds of turbine blades to see which turns fastest. To test your designs fairly, use a fan and make sure you have it on the same speed setting each time. Can you make your turbine lift heavier weights?

LARGER BLADES

To make larger blades for your model, simply use a larger cup.

MORE BLADES

Make a cross out of three lollipop sticks and cut up two cups to make more blades.

HOW IT WORKS

Wind is simply moving air. It is caused by uneven heating of Earth's surface by the Sun. In hot places, the warm air rises, causing cooler air to be drawn into the space left behind, therefore creating wind. For instance, land heats up under the Sun more quickly than the ocean, so on sunny mornings, a breeze often blows from ocean to land. Wind turbines harness the kinetic energy of the wind to cause a generator inside the turbine to make electricity.

High in the sky, air cools down again and begins to sink.

Air over the land warms up and rises.

Cool air flows into the space left by the rising air, creating wind.

Land heats up faster than the ocean.

REAL WORLD: TECHNOLOGY
GENERATING POWER

Wind turbines use the kinetic energy in wind to generate power. Wind causes the turbine's blades to turn, which causes a generator in the main shaft of the turbine to spin. The generator produces electric energy, which can be used to power things. Wind turbines produce the most energy in windy places, such as hilltops and on the coast.

LEVITATING BALL

Levitation is when something is lifted into the air with no visible means of support. Stage magicians pretend they are making things levitate, claiming they are using mysterious magical powers. But it isn't magic—usually a string is holding up the object. But you can make a ping-pong ball levitate with no strings attached and without touching it. It looks like magic, but it's science! The ball is held up by forces working against each other.

A fast jet of air comes from the straw when you blow into the wide tube.

The jet of air supports the ball, even when the ball is not directly over the end of the straw.

HOW TO MAKE A
LEVITATING BALL

To make the ping-pong ball levitate, you need to create a jet of air. In this activity, you do that by blowing into a cardstock tube attached to a piece of drinking straw. For the strongest jet of air, you need to make sure there are no leaks in the tube or straw.

Time
20 minutes

Difficulty
Easy

WHAT YOU NEED

Ruler

Scissors

Felt-tip pen

Pin

Paper straw

Ping-pong ball

Adhesive putty

Colored tape

5½x8½ colored cardstock

Double-sided tape

1 Place a piece of double-sided tape across one of the short edges of the 5½x8½ colored cardstock. Remove the tape's protective strip.

2 Starting at the short edge without the tape on it, roll the cardstock around the felt-tip pen to create a tube. Press the tape down firmly once you reach the end. Remove the pen.

Fold down the tape to form a neat edge, but ensure you keep this end open—don't cover it.

3 Stick down the edge of the cardstock with some colored tape, then wrap more colored tape around one end of the tube.

4 Now close off the other end completely with some more colored tape. This will ensure that no air can escape when you blow into the other end.

5 Use the pin to make a small hole through the colored tape and the cardstock near the closed end of the tube. Gently make the hole a bit bigger with the point of the scissors.

2 in (5 cm)

6 Cut a piece of drinking straw that is about 2 in (5 cm) long. Recycle the rest if you can.

Carefully cut about ½ in (1 cm) into the straw.

7 Carefully make two cuts just over about ½ in (1 cm) long on either side of one end of the straw. Fold up one side in between the two cuts to make a flap.

This flap allows air to flow upward from the tube.

8 Push the cut end of the straw into the hole in the tube, with the flap facing the open end.

9 Use colored tape to secure the flap to the tube, then wrap adhesive putty around the base of the straw where it meets the cardstock tube. Don't press so hard that you close off the airway, but try to block any leaks.

10 Your levitation tube is complete. Hold the ping-pong ball above the straw, blow into the open end of the cardstock tube, and let go of the ball. Can you make the ball levitate?

The air speeds up as it moves from the wide tube to the narrow straw.

HOW IT WORKS

When you blow through the tube, the stream of air pushes the ball, lifting it. Even if you tilt the tube slightly, the ball doesn't drop. This is because air flowing past a smoothly curved object (such as your ball) will curve to flow over its surface and so bend sideways as it leaves. The ball has effectively pushed the airflow sideways, and this results in a "reaction force" that pushes back against the ball. The reaction force stops the ball from falling.

The flowing air "sticks" to the ball and curves around it, creating an area of low pressure.

The jet of air bends sideways.

The ball spins, which helps bend the flowing air.

An area of high pressure pushes back on the ball (the reaction force).

REAL WORLD: SCIENCE
THE POWER OF SAILS

Sails also work by changing the direction of airflow. When wind hits a sail, it follows the curve of the sail, so it is deflected in a different direction. This causes a reaction force that pushes the craft the opposite way. By adjusting the angle of the sail, you can sail in almost any direction—even into the wind!

Turn the handle to lift the load.

The arm at the top of a crane is called a jib.

Marbles hidden inside the stand allow the jib to swing around freely.

The object lifted by the crane is called the load.

LIFTING LOADS

TOWER CRANE

The tall cranes you see on big building sites are called tower cranes. They lift very heavy loads and maneuver them precisely into place while staying perfectly stable. You can explore the science and engineering behind these amazing machines by building your own working model crane.

HOW TO BUILD A
TOWER CRANE

You'll need patience for this build, as there are lots of steps. The trickiest part is the jib—the horizontal arm on top of the crane. It's made of two pieces of cardboard held together by toothpicks. The crane's stand is made from heavier materials that keep the whole structure stable.

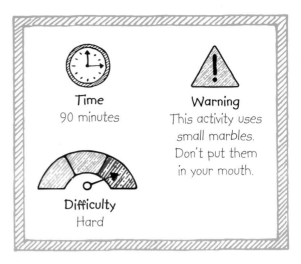

Time
90 minutes

Warning
This activity uses small marbles. Don't put them in your mouth.

Difficulty
Hard

WHAT YOU NEED

Small container

String

Bottle cap

Paint

Duct tape

Toothpicks

Modeling clay

Adhesive putty

Marbles

Two tall paper cups

Clothespin

Scissors

Glue

Pencil

Paintbrushes

Wooden skewer

Large flowerpot and saucer

Sand

Large plastic bottle full of water

Ruler

Thick cardboard
16 x 12 in (40 x 30 cm)

Make sure the bottle fits inside the flowerpot.

2 in
(5 cm)

14 in
(35 cm)

6 in
(15 cm)

1 Use your ruler to draw a 14 in (35 cm) line on a piece of cardboard, near the top. Make pencil marks 2 in (5 cm) and 6 in (15 cm) from the left end of the line.

This line should be 1¼ in (3 cm) long.

3 in
(8 cm)

3 in
(8 cm)

This line should be 1½ in (4 cm) long.

2 Now add four vertical lines: a 1½ in (4 cm) line at the left end, two 3 in (8 cm) lines from your pencil marks, and a 1¼ in (3 cm) line on the right.

Make pencil marks on the second piece, too.

3 Join up the ends of the four vertical lines. The shape you've drawn will form one side of the crane's jib.

4 With scissors, cut out the shape and then use it as a template to make an identical shape on another piece of cardboard.

Add a dot in the middle of the rectangular section.

Be careful of the sharp ends of the toothpicks.

Place adhesive putty under the cardboard to protect the table and your fingers.

5 On one of the shapes, add a dot in the middle of the rectangular section. Draw dots at regular intervals along the edges, as shown above.

6 Stack the two pieces of cardboard together. Using the dots as a guide, carefully push toothpicks through both pieces of cardboard.

First, remove the toothpick from here.

7 Remove the toothpick in the middle of the rectangular section. Carefully pry the two pieces of cardboard apart, keeping them parallel, until just the tips of the toothpicks stick out on both sides.

Friction between the toothpicks and cardboard holds the toothpicks in place until you add glue.

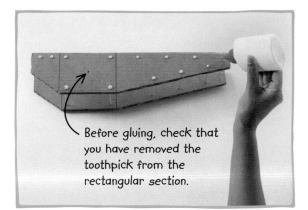

Before gluing, check that you have removed the toothpick from the rectangular section.

8 Dab glue on the tips of the toothpicks. Do this first on one side and let the glue dry. Turn the jib over and do the other side.

9 To make the base of your jib, draw a rectangle on a small piece of cardboard that is 3 in by 4 in (8 cm by 10 cm).

4 in (10 cm)
3 in (8 cm)

10 Turn your jib upside down and put glue on the short horizontal edges. Press the cardboard rectangle into place and let the glue dry.

11 To make your crane's handle, draw two identical circles using the bottle cap as a guide. Carefully cut out the circles.

One of the circles should have a second hole between its middle and edge.

Use adhesive putty to protect the surface.

12 Use a wooden skewer to poke a hole in the middle of each circle. Then, in one of the circles, make an extra hole halfway between the middle and the edge.

Ask an adult to help you if you get stuck.

3½ in (9 cm)   1½ in (4 cm)

13 Measure and cut the skewer into a 3½ in (9 cm) length and a 1½ in (4 cm) length by first scoring it with scissors, then snapping it.

The longer piece goes into the center.

The shorter piece goes into the hole at the side.

The pieces of skewer and cardboard form a device called a crank, which you will use to lift the load.

14 Push the two pieces of wooden skewer into the cardboard circle that has two holes. Glue them in position on both sides.

The second cardboard circle attaches to the other end of the skewer on the other side.

15 Push the long piece of skewer through the hole in the middle of the jib's rectangular section and out the other side. Glue the second cardboard circle to the other end of the skewer.

16 Cover both ends of every toothpick with a small ball of adhesive putty to ensure that no sharp points poke out from the jib.

17 Turn the jib upside down and glue the bottom of one of the paper cups to the base. Wait for the glue to dry.

18 Paint your jib and paper cup. Use whatever colors you like. We've chosen yellow for the main structure and gray for the toothpicks and balls of adhesive putty.

Apply two coats of paint for a good finish.

Tie a knot in the middle of the crank here.

19 Cut 3 ft (1 m) of string and tie one end to the middle of the crank. Thread the other end between the two rows of toothpicks, as shown.

20 Carefully poke the long end of the string through the spring in the clothespin. Tie a knot to hold it in place.

The slabs of modeling clay form a counterweight—a weight that helps balance the load.

21 Make two thick slabs of modeling clay and sandwich them together over the toothpicks at the rear of the jib.

22 Now paint the flowerpot, which will form the crane's heavy base.

23 Take the plastic bottle filled with water and paint it with two coats of paint.

The heavy, sand-filled base keeps the crane stable.

24 Stand the bottle in the flowerpot on top of the saucer and pack sand around it.

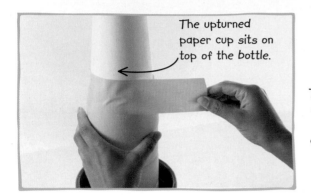

The upturned paper cup sits on top of the bottle.

The marbles will act as bearings—parts in a machine that allow other parts to turn freely.

25 Turn the second paper cup upside down, place it over the bottle, and secure in place with duct tape.

26 Place the marbles inside the lip of the base of the upturned cup. Make sure that there is enough room for the marbles to move a little.

Turn the crank handle to raise and lower the container.

Marbles between the cups act as bearings, reducing friction and allowing the jib to swing around.

Real cranes are anchored to a heavy concrete base for stability. The heavy base of your model does the same job.

27 Mount the crane's jib on the tower by placing the painted cup on top of the marbles. Attach the container with a load inside it to the clothespin and raise or lower it by turning the handle.

The load pulls downward on one side of the crane, exerting a turning force, or torque, on the whole crane.

TEST AND TWEAK

See how heavy a load your crane can lift without toppling over. Try threading the string so it hangs closer to the crane's tower—can the crane lift more now? What happens if you make the wheel of the crank handle bigger, so that your handle moves in a bigger circle? Why not try scaling up the design so that you can lift a heavier load? Or see what happens if you increase or decrease the weight of the counterweight. Perhaps you could use skewers instead of toothpicks, and use a double thickness of cardboard for extra strength.

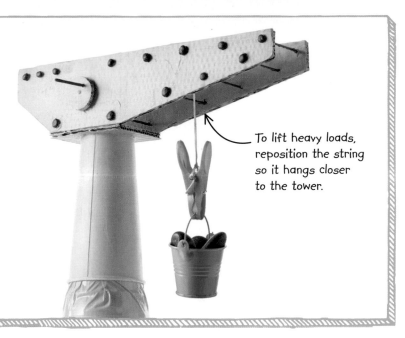

To lift heavy loads, reposition the string so it hangs closer to the tower.

HOW IT WORKS

Tower cranes can lift huge loads without toppling because they can control how far along the jib the load is positioned. Any load pulls downward on the jib, creating a turning force, or torque. The farther along the jib a load is, the greater the torque. (The torque equals the load's weight multiplied by its distance from the tower.) Large loads are lifted close to the tower, and small loads are lifted farther out. As a result, both produce a similar torque, which is roughly balanced by the counterweight. They don't need to be perfectly balanced because the crane is also anchored to the ground.

REAL WORLD: ENGINEERING
CONSTRUCTION CRANES

In a real tower crane, a steel cable hangs from a mobile trolley that can move back and forth along the jib. By varying the position of the trolley, the operator can change the torque created by the load. In your crane, threading the string over different toothpicks does the same thing. A tower crane can lift up to about 22 tons—as much as 20 cars.

Distance A   Distance B

Weight B (load)

Weight A (counterweight)

The crane is perfectly balanced when weight B x distance B = weight A x distance A.

SIMPLE MACHINE
AUTOMATON

An automaton is a mechanical figure that appears to move of its own accord. In reality, automata are powered by hand, clockwork, or electric motors. Automata date back more than 2,000 years and were often built to entertain audiences. In this project, you can make a shark automaton that swishes its tail and opens its jaws. These movements are controlled by devices called cams and cranks, which are found in many kinds of machines, including car engines.

The jaw moves up and down.

This wooden skewer forms a push rod—a straight piece that is pushed up and down.

Twisting this skewer around transfers energy to the cam, which transfers it to the shark's mouth, making it open and close.

This circular piece of cardboard is a cam. It rotates off-center on the skewer, causing the push rod to move up and down.

The skewer attached to the tail moves backward and forward in an arc (a part of a circle).

This handle turns a crank that makes the shark's tail flex back and forth.

HOW TO MAKE AN
AUTOMATON

This challenging build will take you a while. You'll need plenty of thick cardboard, as this project has lots of small pieces. You can still do this activity if you don't have a cardboard box exactly the same size as ours, but you may have to adjust some of the other pieces you cut.

Time
120 minutes

Difficulty
Hard

WHAT YOU NEED

Paint

Colored tape

Scissors

Pencil

Paper straw

String

Paintbrushes

Adhesive putty

Ruler

Five wooden skewers

Glue

Paperclip

Lots of thick cardboard

Colored paper

Cardboard box
11 in x 6 in x 3 in
(26 cm x 16 cm x 8 cm)

Double-sided tape

1 To make the base of your automaton, draw a rectangle 8 in by 6 in (20 cm by 15 cm) on a small piece of thick cardboard.

2 On another small piece of cardboard, draw a second rectangle 5 in by 6 in (12 cm by 15 cm). Cut out both rectangles.

3 Apply double-sided tape across the middle and around the edges of the larger rectangle. Peel the protective strip off the tape.

The base attaches to the long side of the box.

4 Stick the two rectangles together, as shown, leaving part of the large rectangle exposed. Place the long side of the box onto the exposed part.

Each mark should be ¾ in (2 cm) from the edge of the box.

The pencil line will act as a guide for where to insert the wooden skewers.

5 On the top, make three marks ¾ in (2 cm) from the edge in the middle and at both ends. Draw a straight pencil line to join them.

6 To make the mechanism for the automaton's right-hand section, draw two 5 by ¾ in (12 by 2 cm) rectangles on cardboard. Cut them out.

Hold the cardboard next to the ruler as you mark it.

7 Make three dots along the middle of one of the small rectangles, ¾ in, 1½ in, and 3 in (2 cm, 4 cm, and 8 cm) from one end.

8 On the other small rectangle, make two pencil dots along the middle, ½ in (1 cm) from each end.

Use adhesive putty to protect the table.

9 Using a wooden *skewer*, make holes in the dots you made on the small rectangles.

Put adhesive putty on the other side of the card to protect your fingers.

6 in (15 cm)

10 Push the *skewer* through the top of the box 6 in (15 cm) in from the left, then through the hole in the rectangle with three holes, as shown. Poke the *skewer* into the *base* of the box and glue it.

Ask an adult to help if you find this part tricky.

This is the 2 in (5 cm) piece of *skewer*.

11 Take another *skewer* and make marks 2 in, 4 in, and 5½ in (5 cm, 10 cm, and 13 cm) along it. Use scissors to *score* and *break* it at each mark.

12 Push the 2 in (5 cm) piece of *skewer* through the middle hole. Place a full-length *skewer* through the remaining hole.

The distance between the *skewer* and pencil should be 2½ in (6 cm).

The handle will be placed on top of this piece of *skewer*.

4 in (10 cm)

13 Push the 1¼ in (3 cm) piece of *skewer* into the base so that it is 4 in (10 cm) away from and in line with the *skewer* that goes through the top of the box. Add glue.

14 Use a short piece of string tied to a pencil to draw an arc around the *skewer* that goes through the top of the box. Cut out a ½ in (1 cm) wide *slit* along the arc.

The circle should be about 1½ in (4 cm) wide.

Take care when using scissors.

15 To make the handle for the right-hand section of the automaton, draw around a roll of tape on cardboard to make a circle. Cut it out.

16 Cut a 1½ in (4 cm) length of straw. Cut four slits at one end and fold them out. Glue these flaps down onto the cardboard circle.

The small rectangle acts as a crank. It turns the handle's rotation movement into a back-and-forth motion.

17 Push the remaining 2 in (5 cm) piece of skewer into the handle close to the edge of the circle. Turn the handle over and place the straw over the small piece of skewer you stuck to the base. Put the spare rectangle from step 9 over the two small pieces of skewer, as shown.

The shark's body is in four separate pieces.

This dot marks where the hinge for your shark's jaw will go.

5 in (12 cm)

2½ in (6½ cm)

3 in (7½ cm)

4 in (10 cm)

Notice the hook in the shark's lower jaw.

18 On another piece of cardboard, draw a shark like the one here for the top of your automaton. The shark should be about three-quarters the length of your box. Cut out the pieces of the shark.

This paper backing will allow the shark's body to move freely once it is attached to the skewers.

Top jaw

³/₄ in (2 cm)

³/₄ in (2 cm)

Don't put double-sided tape in the gaps.

19 Place the three shark pieces shown above on colored paper, with gaps of about ³/₄ in (2 cm) between them. Draw around them and join the gaps to create the outline shown.

20 Cut out the paper shape. Attach the pieces of the shark's body to the paper using double-sided tape. Be sure to leave ³/₄ in (2 cm) gaps between the top jaw, the middle, and the tail.

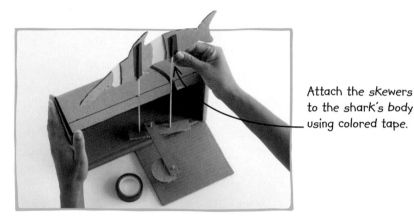

Attach the skewers to the shark's body using colored tape.

21 Use tape to attach the shark's body and tail to the two skewers that are sticking up from the box. Cut off any excess bits of skewer that stick out above the shark.

22 You now need to add a wall to divide your automaton into two sections. To do this, measure and cut a rectangle that matches the depth and height of your box.

3½ in (9 cm)

This section will house the mechanism for your shark's jaw.

This circle will form part of a cam—a device that turns circular motion into up-and-down motion.

The circle should be about 1½ in (3½ cm) wide.

23 Glue the rectangle of cardboard 3½ in (9 cm) from the left side of the box. Make sure it doesn't prevent the mechanism on the right from moving freely back and forth.

24 To make the mechanism for your automaton's left-hand section, draw a small circle on a piece of cardboard, using the inside of the colored tape as a guide, and cut it out.

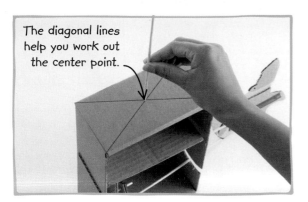

The diagonal lines help you work out the center point.

25 Turn the box on its right side and draw diagonal lines across the top end to find the center. Push the pointed end of a skewer through the point where the diagonal lines meet.

In order to make the cam work, the skewer is off-center.

26 Turn the box back on its base. Push the skewer through the circle about ½ in (1 cm) from its edge. Gently push the skewer's tip through the cardboard wall.

Fold along the dotted line.

27 Now draw and cut out a 1½ in by 2½ in (4 cm by 6 cm) rectangle and fold it in half lengthwise.

This is a push rod. The cam pushes it up and down.

28 Push a skewer through the center of the folded cardboard rectangle so that it just pokes through. Add a dab of glue and let it dry.

29 Make a hole on the pencil line that lines up with the middle of the jaw. Push a 2 in (5 cm) piece of straw through the hole, then insert the push rod by feeding it up through the straw.

This small circle will keep the lower jaw from wobbling.

30 To make the hinge for the jaw, cut out a cardboard circle ¾ in (2 cm) wide. Push a short piece of skewer through this and through the dot in the upper jaw. Hook the lower jaw in between.

Trim the skewer here.

Rest this cardboard on the circular cam below.

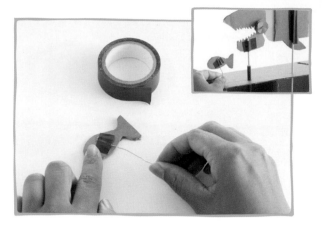

31 Tape the push rod to the shark's lower jaw, making sure the folded piece of cardboard is resting on the cam inside the box. Cut off any excess bits of skewer.

32 To decorate your automaton, draw a fish onto a small piece of cardboard and cut it out. Straighten a paperclip, tape one end to the fish, and stick the other into the top of the box.

33 Finally, paint your automaton as you like. To make your automaton work, turn the handle to swish the shark's tail and twist the skewer at the side of the box to make the jaw move up and down.

The tail moves side to side.

The lower jaw moves up and down.

Push rod

Twisting this skewer causes the cam to rotate, moving the push rod up and down.

If the skewer slips, add glue where it passes through the cardboard circle.

Decorate the various parts of your automaton as you like.

Crank

Turning the handle causes the crank to move back and forth and the shark's tail to swish.

HOW IT WORKS

When you twirl the skewer at the left side of the automaton, it turns the cam—the cardboard circle that is set off-center on the skewer. The cam pushes a folded rectangle and the push rod up and down as it rotates, turning circular motion into up-and-down motion.

In the right-hand section the arm attached to the circle is a crank. As the handle turns, one end of the crank moves around with it, pivoting as it goes and pushing the other end in and out. A crank can turn rotation into back-and-forth motion or do the opposite, turning back-and-forth motion into rotation.

LEFT-HAND MECHANISM

Push rod

The push rod moves up and down as the cam turns.

Cam

Fixed point

Fixed point

The skewer is off-center.

Fixed point

RIGHT-HAND MECHANISM

Fixed point

Fixed point

Handle

Fixed point

As you turn the handle, the circle rotates.

Handle

Fixed point

The crank converts the circular motion of the handle into back-and-forth motion.

Fixed point

Fixed point

Handle

Fixed point

Fixed point

Handle

REAL WORLD: TECHNOLOGY
CAR ENGINE

Cranks and cams are very important components in most car engines. Pistons push up or down inside the engine, and cranks turn that motion into circular motion that turns the wheels. A set of cams on a shaft open and close valves that allow gasoline vapor into the engine and exhaust gases out at just the right moments.

Camshaft

Cam

Valve

Piston

Crank

Crankshaft

LIQUIDS AND REACTIONS

Getting to know the properties of everyday liquids such as water and oils is a great way to learn about science. In this chapter, you'll turn your kitchen into a chemistry lab. You'll investigate how to keep liquids cool, as well as how to warm them up, and experiment with chemical reactions using a variety of household substances, including vinegar and cabbage juice. You'll also explore the science behind gels and smells by creating your own air freshener.

The temperature inside your body is around 99°F (37°C). When your surroundings are colder than that, you lose heat through your skin.

With a layer of oil between your skin and the cold water in this activity, your hand will lose heat much more slowly.

MATERIAL INSULATION
BLUBBER GLOVE

If you swam in the icy cold waters of the oceans in the Arctic or Antarctic, your warm body would quickly lose heat. One way you could slow down that heat loss would be to wear a suit that contained a layer of oil or fat. The suit would work just like the fatty *blubber* that whales, dolphins, and seals have to protect them from the cold. Materials that protect against the cold are known as insulation.

HOW TO MAKE A

BLUBBER GLOVE

For this activity, you need to create a layer of vegetable oil or sunflower oil next to your skin before plunging your hand into icy water. You'll be doing that by making a two-layer glove using plastic bags. When you've finished with the oil, find a good way to dispose of it—don't pour it down the sink, as it might cause a clog!

Time
15 minutes

Difficulty
Easy

WHAT YOU NEED

Vegetable or sunflower oil

Scissors

Duct tape

Two small plastic bags (with zipper seals)

Funnel

Large bowl or bucket of icy water

Timer

1 Turn one of the small plastic bags inside out by reaching inside it and pulling the bottom out through the top. Straighten the bag out.

2 Put your hand inside the inside-out bag and then put it into the other plastic bag. The zipper on the inner bag faces outward, and the zipper on the outer bag faces inward.

This gap is where you will pour in the oil.

3 Press the zippers on the two bags together to create a seal. Make sure you leave one part unsealed.

4 Apply tape to the parts of the bags you have zipped together and fold it over to seal them together. Do not put tape over the gap you left.

Ask for help if you find it difficult to hold the bag, the funnel, and the bottle of oil.

5 Put the funnel's spout into the gap *between* the bags. Carefully pour in enough oil to fill the bag two-thirds full.

The tape will keep any oil from leaking.

6 Zip the gap up and use another piece of tape to cover it, sealing in the oil. Fold over the tape.

7 Hold one hand under the icy water and time how long you can leave it in there before it becomes uncomfortable.

8 Wait a few minutes for your hand to return to normal temperature, then put it inside the inner bag. Now plunge your hand, inside the *blubber* glove, into the icy water. Time how long you can keep your hand in the water now, and compare it to the time you recorded before.

Vegetable oil is made of chemical compounds called fats, just like the fatty tissue that whales, dolphins, and seals have.

Make sure no cold water spills into the glove.

TEST AND TWEAK

Nerve endings in your skin give you your sense of hot and cold. They don't detect actual temperatures—instead, they sense the loss or gain of heat from your skin.

Cold water / Lukewarm water / Warm water

1 Fill one bowl with cold water, one with lukewarm water, and one with warm water. Keep one hand in cold water for a few seconds, so that it cools down, and the other in warm water, so that it warms up.

2 Put both hands in lukewarm water. The hand that was in cold water will feel warm, while the hand that was in warm water will feel cold, as heat flows either to or from each hand.

HOW IT WORKS

When you plunge your hand into the icy water, heat flows quickly from your skin to the water, and you feel the cold within seconds. When you use the blubber glove, the layer of oil around your hand slows down that loss of heat because heat flows more slowly through the oil. Materials through which heat passes slowly are called insulators. Like oil, air is a good insulator. Wool sweaters trap lots of air, which is why they are good at keeping you warm on a winter's day.

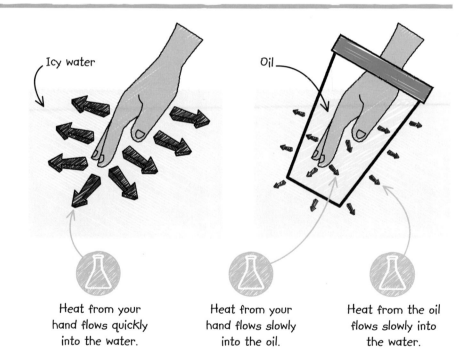

Icy water

Oil

Heat from your hand flows quickly into the water.

Heat from your hand flows slowly into the oil.

Heat from the oil flows slowly into the water.

REAL WORLD: SCIENCE
BLUBBERY ANIMALS

Whales, dolphins, and seals are mammals. That means they are warm blooded. In order to survive in the icy Arctic or Antarctic, where water temperatures are extremely cold, these animals have a thick layer of fatty tissue called blubber. Blubber slows down the loss of heat from their bodies. A blue whale's blubber layer is 12 in (30 cm) thick!

THERMOS

If you're having a picnic on a hot day, it's a real treat to be able to have a cool drink. But if you carry a cold drink in an ordinary bottle, the Sun's heat and the warm air will gradually warm it up. You can keep cold drinks cold for longer by carrying them in a thermos. A thermos reduces the transfer of heat, so it keeps hot drinks hot and cold drinks cold for longer.

The foil helps prevent heat from reaching or leaving the drink inside.

There's a gap between the two bottles in this thermos that reduces the transfer of heat to or from the drink inside.

HOW TO MAKE A
THERMOS

You'll make your thermos with two bottles—a glass one to hold the drink and a larger plastic one. It might be a bit difficult to get bottles that nest together well, but try to find a glass bottle that is slightly smaller than the plastic one—it is important that there is a gap between the two bottles.

Time
30 minutes

Difficulty
Medium

WHAT YOU NEED

Ruler

Two glasses

Measuring cup and ice water

Funnel

Scissors

Colored tape

Adhesive putty

Aluminum foil

Glass bottle

Plastic bottle

Thermometer

1 With scissors, carefully make a hole about ½ in (1 cm) down from the bottle cap. Cut the top off the bottle. Ask an adult if you find this tricky.

2 Cut around the middle of the bottle. You should end up with three parts: the very top, with the cap, and the top and bottom halves of the bottle.

3 Stick a lump of adhesive putty on top of the bottle cap, then push the upside-down cap into the bottom of the plastic bottle.

4 Cut a piece of aluminum foil about 12 in (30 cm) long and wrap it around the glass bottle, including the bottom, so no glass is visible.

5 Put the glass bottle on top of the upturned bottle cap inside the plastic bottle. Slip the top half of the plastic bottle over, then tape the two halves back together.

6 Tape the neck of the plastic bottle to the neck of the glass bottle to create a seal.

7 To insulate the top of your thermos, cut a piece of aluminum foil about 8 in (20 cm) long. Fold the foil in half lengthwise and then in half again to create a thick piece.

8 Wrap the thick piece of foil around the bottle cap of the glass bottle.

9 Pour some ice water into a glass and set aside. Remove the cap of your thermos and pour in ice water from a measuring cup using a funnel. Put the cap back on.

The funnel will keep water from spilling down the sides of the thermos.

Compare the temperature of this glass of water to the temperature of the water from the thermos.

Reflective materials reflect invisible infrared radiation, as well as light.

10 After about an hour, pour some water from the thermos into another glass. Compare its temperature to the temperature of the water in the other glass.

HOW IT WORKS

Leave a glass of ice water at room temperature, and the water will slowly warm up. Heat enters the water in two ways: conduction and radiation. Conduction is the transfer of heat between two things that are in contact. Your thermos greatly reduces this effect because the air gap insulates the ice water inside the glass bottle. Invisible infrared radiation also warms the water, but these rays are reflected by the metal foil. The air and foil can prevent heat from being lost from warm liquids, too.

Infrared radiation from sources such as the Sun passes through the plastic but is reflected by the foil.

The bottle cap and the air gap help to reduce heat conduction.

REAL WORLD: TECHNOLOGY

In thermos flasks you buy at the store, the air is removed from the gap between the inner compartment and the outer surface, which creates a vacuum. The vacuum reduces heat transfer to or from the liquid inside to almost nothing. This makes it possible to keep liquids very cold or hot for long periods.

Vacuum gap

Inner compartment

The water level drops as water flows through the straw.

The pressure of the water in the cup pushes water up and over the bend in the straw.

PYTHAGORAS CUP

This strange-looking contraption is named after the Greek mathematician Pythagoras, who lived 2,000 years ago. Pythagoras's cup was designed to catch greedy people who tried to take more than their fair share of wine. When filled above a certain point, the cup drains the liquid (in this case, water) through its base. It works because a liquid will always flow from an area of high pressure to an area of low pressure—an effect known as a siphon.

The water keeps on flowing until the cup is nearly empty.

HOW TO MAKE A
PYTHAGORAS CUP

This activity can be a bit complicated, but the surprising result is worth it, so please be patient and follow the instructions carefully. To make the Pythagoras cup, you'll need to use a lot of plastic. Make sure you recycle it once you're finished.

Time
20 minutes

Difficulty
Medium

WHAT YOU NEED

Ruler

Pencil

Bendy plastic straw

Scissors

Food coloring

Bowl of water

Plastic cup

Rubber band

Adhesive putty

Colored tape

Plastic bottle

Dish

1 Cut around the bottle, about 2¾ in (7 cm) from the top, and keep the top part. Cover any sharp or uneven parts of the cut edge with tape.

Adhesive putty

2 Remove the bottle's cap and use the scissors to make a hole in it. Place the cap on top of a lump of adhesive putty to protect the table.

3 Press the lump of adhesive putty onto the top of the cap. With scissors, make a hole in it, in line with the hole in the cap.

The bend should be at this end.

The rubber band will ensure the fold is held close together, but not too tight.

4 Cut about 1 in (2 cm) off the end of the straw farthest from the bendy part. Fold the straw at its bendy part and secure it in place by wrapping it with a rubber band.

5 Make a hole in the middle of the bottom of the plastic cup. Use a lump of adhesive putty underneath the cup to protect the table.

The adhesive putty acts as a seal to stop any leaks.

6 Feed the long end of the folded straw through the hole in the plastic cup, making sure that the folded part is inside the cup.

7 Push the long end of the straw through the hole in the adhesive putty and the bottle cap.

Use a pencil to pack the putty around the straw to create a seal.

8 Push the adhesive putty on the bottle cap onto the bottom of the plastic cup. Use a pencil to pack some more adhesive putty around the straw on the inside of the top of the bottle.

9 Pour some food coloring into the water. Stand the plastic cup inside the dish. Begin pouring the water into the cup.

Food coloring makes it easier to see the water.

The bottle cap acts as a base for the Pythagoras cup.

10 The cup will fill up until the level of the water reaches above the top of the straw. When it does, all the water will leak out!

TEST AND TWEAK

You can explore this effect with two bendy straws, two glasses (one tall, one short), and water. Make a long tube by pushing one straw into the other. Fill the tall glass with water and bend the tube so that the short end of the tube is in the tall glass. Suck a little water out through the long end to start the flow, then let the long end rest in the short glass. Water will drain from the glass until the water level goes down to the opening of the straw.

Use a piece of tape to connect the straws.

You might need a base to make your tall glass taller.

HOW IT WORKS

When you're filling the cup, water climbs up the straw, pushed by the pressure of the water, which increases as more water is poured in. When the water level in the cup is greater than the height of the straw, the pressure pushes water over the top of the bent part of the straw. The water keeps flowing, because the pressure at the bend in the straw remains lower than the pressure at the open part of the straw inside the cup. This effect is known as a siphon.

The water climbs over the bend in the straw, then starts to drain out of the cup.

Water is pushed up inside the straw.

Water continues to drain out of the cup until it is empty.

REAL WORLD: SCIENCE
TOILET FLUSH

You probably use a siphon most days—when you flush the toilet. The box at the top of the toilet is called a cistern. Inside, water fills up to just above the level of a pipe that leads down into the toilet bowl. When you turn the handle, you release water into that pipe, and all the water from the cistern rushes into the bowl.

AIR FRESHENER

Natural soaps and perfumes often get their scents from essential oils—concentrated liquids (essences) extracted from plants. Some people put drops of essential oil on small dishes so the scent fills a room as the oil molecules evaporate (turn to gas). But once all the oil has evaporated, the wonderful aroma disappears. In these air fresheners, essential oils are held in a jellylike substance called a gel. They evaporate more slowly, so they can make your room smell great for weeks.

Inside the jar is a gel—a substance that is mostly liquid but holds its shape like a solid.

For a decorative flourish, immerse cut flowers or other ornaments in your jars of jelly.

A small amount of food coloring makes the gel look more attractive.

HOW TO MAKE AN
AIR FRESHENER

For this activity, you need a gelling agent, which is what cooks use to make jelly. Gelling agents that work well include carrageenan and gelatin. Whatever you use, check the instructions on the packet so you make it correctly. You'll also need an essential oil. Any kind will work, but choose one you like the smell of!

1 Add one level teaspoon of gelling agent to the glass jar.

Time
15 minutes

Difficulty
Easy

Warning
Hot water! Adult supervision required.

WHAT YOU NEED

Teaspoon of gelling agent

Teaspoon of salt

Measuring cup of hot water

Glass jar

Food coloring

Essential oil

2 Add hot water until the jar is two-thirds full. Stir with the teaspoon until the gelling agent dissolves. Take care to avoid splashing as you stir.

3 Add a few drops of food coloring to give your mixture a bit of color. Mix it in with the teaspoon.

Salt acts as a preservative—it prevents bacteria and fungi from growing on the gel.

4 Now for the freshening part. Add a few drops of an essential oil and stir the mixture again.

5 Add a teaspoon of salt and stir well until it completely dissolves.

The mixture will set in the fridge and become a gel.

6 Place the mixture in the fridge overnight to cool down and set. It's now ready to use! After 2–3 weeks, dispose of the air freshener.

TEST AND TWEAK

The rate at which substances evaporate depends on the temperature. To investigate, place your air freshener in warm and cold places. Where is the smell strongest? Add flowers, marbles, or polished pebbles before the gel sets to make the air freshener look nicer. If you use flowers, dispose of your air freshener after about a week, before they get moldy.

HOW IT WORKS

Gelling agents contain long, chainlike molecules called polymers. When they dissolve in hot water and then cool down, they form crosslinks with each other, creating a three-dimensional scaffold that holds water in place and keeps its shape—a gel. The essential oil also gets trapped in the gel. As a result, it evaporates into the air more slowly, keeping your room smelling fresh for weeks.

Polymer molecules

Dry gelling agent

Dissolved in hot water

After cooling

Crosslinks between molecules

REAL WORLD: SCIENCE
CONTACT LENSES

Soft contact lenses are made from a gel containing water and plastic. As well as making them comfortable, the gel allows oxygen to pass through to the eye's surface. That's important because the eye has no blood vessels and gets all its oxygen from the air.

ACID AND BASE REACTION
BUBBLE TOWER

Turn your kitchen into a chemistry lab! At the heart of this activity is a chemical reaction between two substances: one called an acid (you'll use vinegar) and one called a base (in this case, baking soda). The reaction produces amazing bubbles that rise through a tower of oil and then fall back down. So that the effect is even more impressive, you'll also make an indicator—a color-changing solution that turns red in acids and blue-green in bases—using some red cabbage.

The bubbles produced by the reaction float up through oil.

The pink solution at the bottom of the vase contains an acid and a pH indicator.

A chemical reaction at the bottom of the glass produces bubbles.

HOW TO MAKE A
BUBBLE TOWER

The first thing you'll need to do is to make the pH indicator. This involves soaking pieces of red cabbage in warm water. Once you've done this, you'll add vinegar, which is an acid. You'll then carry out the reaction in a vase, which makes it easy to watch the colorful bubbles rise and fall. When you've finished, put the oil in the trash, not down the sink.

Time
15 minutes

Difficulty
Easy

WHAT YOU NEED

Measuring cup

½ red cabbage

Scissors

Small bowl

Spoon

Baking soda

Distilled vinegar

Vegetable or sunflower oil

Vase or tall glass

Large bowl

Sieve

1 Half-fill the small bowl with warm water. Cut thin strips off the red cabbage, letting them fall into the water. Let stand for 10 minutes until the water turns a deep purple color.

2 Pour the mixture through the sieve into the large bowl. Put the cabbage leaves into a food recycling bin or the trash.

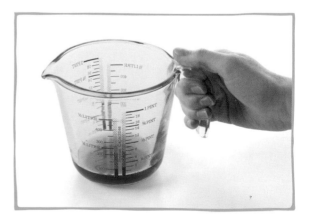

3 Pour 2 fl oz (50 ml) of the purple solution into the measuring cup. This solution is your pH indicator.

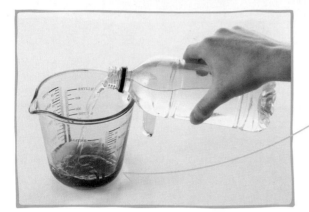

Your pH indicator changes color when mixed with an acidic substance.

4 Now add 2 fl oz (50 ml) of vinegar to your pH indicator. Don't take your eyes off the cup—the solution will turn bright pink almost instantly! It turns pink because of the vinegar's acidity.

5 Spoon baking soda into the vase or tall glass. Add enough to cover its base.

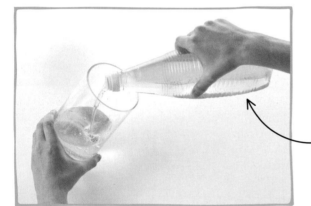

Pour the oil gently so it doesn't stir up the baking soda.

6 Pour oil over the baking soda. You need to add enough oil to fill the vase about two-thirds full.

7 Slowly pour the pink vinegar into the vase. As soon as the vinegar meets the baking soda, you'll see red bubbles rise up through the oil. Watch what happens over the next few minutes. As the reaction continues, the bubbles will change color as the acidity of the liquid inside them changes.

The oil is less dense than the vinegar, so it floats on top.

A chemical reaction between the acid and base creates bubbles of carbon dioxide gas.

TEST AND TWEAK

Why not try mixing your red cabbage indicator with other substances to see if it will change to any other colors? Ask an adult to help you, because some of the chemicals you find in the home can be harmful if they splash on you—especially in your eyes. Also, never put any household product in your mouth. Try the following: bottled water, lemonade, liquid soap, baking powder, or lemon juice.

Scientists use indicators to measure how acidic or basic a solution is on a scale from 0 to 14. This is called the pH scale. Acids have a pH of less than 7, and bases have a pH of more than 7. Water, which is neither acidic nor basic, is called "neutral" and has a pH of 7. The cabbage-water indicator is red in acids, is purple in neutral solutions, and turns blue-green or even green in strong bases.

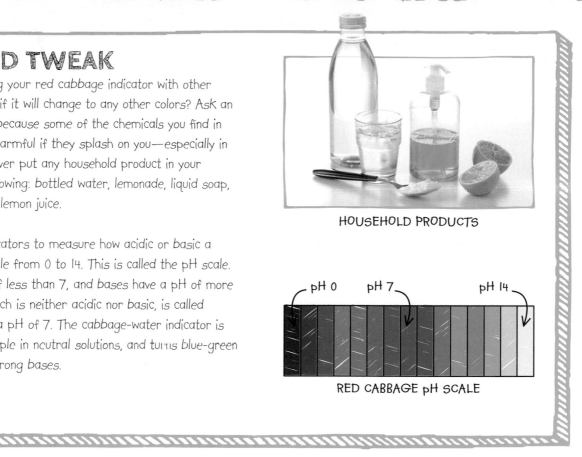

HOUSEHOLD PRODUCTS

pH 0   pH 7   pH 14

RED CABBAGE pH SCALE

HOW IT WORKS

The vinegar solution is acidic. It is also more dense than the oil, so it sinks when you pour it into the vase. The acid reacts with the baking soda, producing bubbles of carbon dioxide gas (mixed with vinegar solution), which are less dense than the oil and rise up. At the surface, the bubbles burst and any vinegar solution inside them drops down. The purple pigment in red cabbage is an indicator—a chemical that changes color depending on how acidic a solution is. At first it is pink, but it turns blue-green as the acid is used up in the reaction.

Oil

Bubbles float to the top.

Bubbles of carbon dioxide are produced by the reaction.

Vinegar sinks below the oil.

Baking soda reacts with vinegar.

REAL WORLD: TECHNOLOGY
BAKING CUPCAKES

You might have used baking powder to make cupcakes. Baking powder is baking soda mixed with a powdered acid. When it's added to a cupcake mixture, it gets wet, and the chemicals dissolve and begin to react. Heat speeds up the reaction, producing large bubbles of carbon dioxide that make the cupcakes rise as they bake.

COPPER COATING

COPPER REACTIONS

Set up your own chemistry lab in the kitchen! Using just vinegar, salt, some pennies, and a steel nail, you can observe some amazing chemical reactions. The pennies will become shiny and new, and the steel nail will become copper-plated and change color.

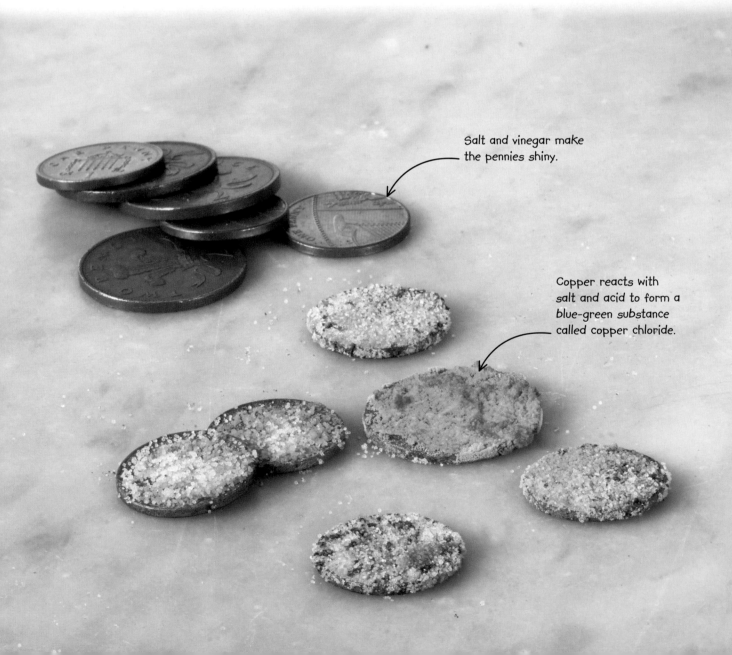

Salt and vinegar make the pennies shiny.

Copper reacts with salt and acid to form a blue-green substance called copper chloride.

The steel nail is coated with copper.

A copper-coated coin reacts with salt and vinegar to produce a green solution.

HOW TO MAKE
COPPER REACTIONS

The vinegar used in these three experiments is a weak acid. It won't harm you if it gets on your skin, but if you splash some in your eyes, it will sting. If that happens, just rinse your eyes with cold water. If you spill the vinegar or the salt, just wipe them up with a paper towel.

Time
40 minutes

Warning
Be careful not to get vinegar in your eyes.

Difficulty
Medium

WHAT YOU NEED

Ungalvanized steel nail

10 pennies

Glass bowl

Teaspoon

Table salt

Measuring cup

Plastic bowl

Ceramic bowl

Paper towel

Distilled vinegar

EXPERIMENT 1—SHINY PENNIES

1 Put 10 pennies in the glass bowl.

The pennies are not copper all the way through, but they are coated with copper.

2 Pour enough vinegar into the bowl to cover the pennies. Vinegar contains a chemical called acetic acid, which will react with the pennies.

The chlorine in salt helps the acid dissolve the copper on the pennies.

3 Now stir in half a teaspoon of salt and leave for 10 minutes. Salt is made of the elements sodium and chlorine.

4 The pennies will have turned shiny and bright. Take them out of the vinegar and salt solution. Keep them close by in a bowl.

HOW IT WORKS

Everything around you is made of tiny particles called atoms. Atoms of different kinds (elements) join together in different ways, forming compounds. In a chemical reaction, atoms can separate, swap partners, and form new compounds. Pennies are shiny when new but turn dull brown over time because the copper atoms react with

oxygen atoms from the air to form a compound called copper oxide. Vinegar contains a compound called acetic acid, which splits in water to release positively charged hydrogen atoms (hydrogen ions). These react with the copper oxide, stripping it from the pennies and revealing the shiny layer of pure copper underneath. Salt speeds up this reaction.

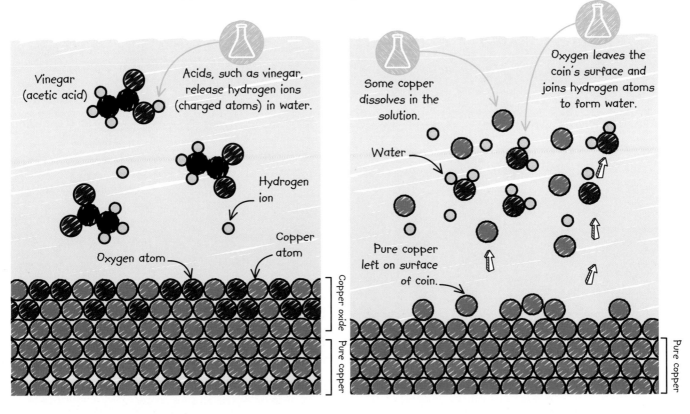

Vinegar (acetic acid)

Acids, such as vinegar, release hydrogen ions (charged atoms) in water.

Hydrogen ion

Oxygen atom

Copper atom

Copper oxide   Pure copper

Some copper dissolves in the solution.

Oxygen leaves the coin's surface and joins hydrogen atoms to form water.

Water

Pure copper left on surface of coin.

Pure copper

EARLY STAGE OF THE REACTION

LATER STAGE OF THE REACTION

EXPERIMENT 2—COPPER PLATING

1 For the next experiment, use the vinegar and salt solution from the first experiment. It contains the copper from the pennies. Put the *steel* nail into the solution.

The nail is now copper-plated.

2 After about 20 minutes, your nail should have changed color. The copper from the pennies now coats the nail.

HOW IT WORKS

Steel is a mixture of several different elements, but is made mostly of iron. Some of the iron atoms from the nail's surface dissolve in the solution—and some of the copper atoms from the solution (which originally came from the surface of the pennies) attach to the nail instead. That's why the nail turns copper-colored.

1. Copper atoms from the solution attach to the nail's surface.

2. Some iron breaks away and dissolves in the solution.

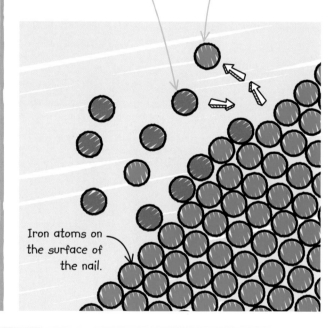

Iron atoms on the surface of the nail.

TEST AND TWEAK

Why not study in more detail the reactions between vinegar, salt, and copper? You can do this by letting the reactions go on for longer. Here are some of the stages of the reaction you might see.

1 Pour 2 fl oz (50 ml) of vinegar into the cup. Add half a teaspoon of salt. Stir until the salt is dissolved.

2 Put a coin in a jar and add the solution. Put the lid on. Leave it for a few days, opening daily to let in air.

EXPERIMENT 3—MAKING COPPER CHLORIDE

1 Place a folded piece of paper towel into the plastic bowl. Soak the paper towel with vinegar.

2 Put one of the pennies into the bowl with the vinegar-soaked paper towel.

3 Spoon salt on top of the penny until the coin is completely covered.

The copper reacts with chlorine atoms from salt to form copper (II) chloride, which is blue-green.

4 Leave it for about an hour or two. You should see a green coating of copper chloride. Wash your hands after touching the coin.

HOW IT WORKS

When you leave a penny covered with salt and vinegar for a long time, a chemical reaction takes place. Salt is made of the elements sodium and chlorine. The chlorine reacts with the copper, producing a chemical compound called basic copper (II) chloride. This compound has a bright blue-green color.

1. The solution contains chlorine atoms from the dissolved salt.

2. Chlorine and copper atoms combine to form copper (II) chloride.

Copper atoms join with chlorine atoms to form green copper (II) chloride.

As time passes and more air is let in, the solution turns brown.

Finally, the solution becomes clear, but sooty deposits of copper (II) oxide can be seen in it.

SHAPES AND STRUCTURES

A building or a bridge needs to be strong enough to stay standing, and it also needs to hold up anything placed in or on top of it. But what makes a structure strong enough to support loads? It's all down to what it is made from, what shape it is, and how it's built. In this chapter, you'll be building some surprisingly strong structures using paper, sand, and drinking straws. You'll even build tall towers from spaghetti and marshmallows!

CONSTRUCTION SCIENCE
SPAGHETTI TOWER

For a tower to stay standing, it must be strong enough not to buckle under its own weight, and it must have a stable base. This tower is strong because of the shapes used in its construction: triangles. And its wide base keeps it from toppling.

The tower must stand straight, or the force of gravity will tip it over.

Triangles are strong because they can't twist out of shape.

The main part of the tower is made of two large cubes stacked together.

The base carries all the tower's weight.

HOW TO MAKE A
SPAGHETTI TOWER

All you need to build this tower is spaghetti, marshmallows, and willpower! The sticky marshmallows hold the ends of the spaghetti in place, and the spaghetti forms a sturdy framework. If you like marshmallows, you'll need willpower to stop yourself from eating your building materials!

Time
20 minutes

Difficulty
Medium

WHAT YOU NEED

Marshmallows

Uncooked spaghetti

1 Begin by making a square. To see why a square isn't a strong shape, push it gently from one side. It leans easily, becoming a parallelogram.

Make sure the bottom marshmallows sit on their flat bases.

2 Make a cube. Try twisting it gently. Because it's made of squares, you'll find it leans very easily and isn't stable.

Sliding the marshmallows inward helps to make the cube stronger.

3 To make the cube stronger, you'll need to add diagonal pieces. To fit them, first make the cube smaller by sliding the marshmallows inward so the spaghetti strands poke out the other side.

The diagonal pieces keep the cube from leaning.

4 Add the diagonal pieces, called braces, across each face from corner to corner.

Diagonal braces strengthen the square sides by creating triangle shapes.

5 Strengthen the vertical edges by feeding a second piece of spaghetti down through the marshmallows at the top corners.

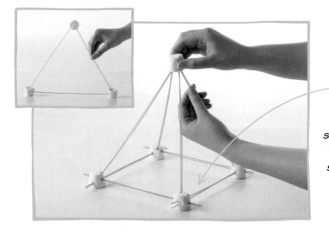

Make sure the square base of the roof is the same size as the top of your cube.

6 Make the roof, starting with a triangle. You'll notice this is stronger than a square, as it doesn't lean. Add more spaghetti and marshmallows to form a pyramid with a square base.

7 Build a second braced cube and fit it very carefully on top of the first one. Then, just as carefully, fit the pyramid on top. Your tower is now complete!

Push the base of the top cube onto the bits of spaghetti sticking up from the first one.

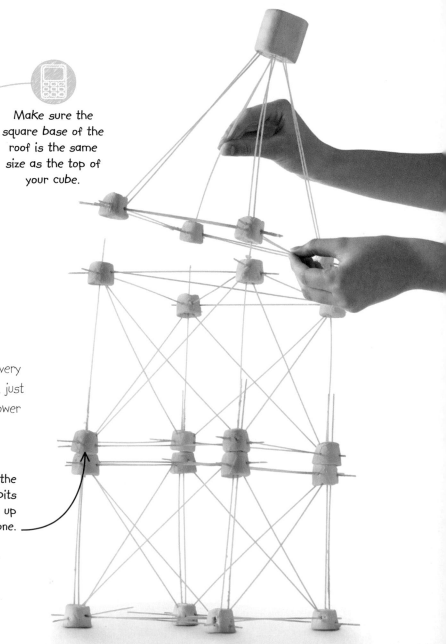

TEST AND TWEAK

Now that you've mastered the art of building spaghetti towers, why not try different designs? You could try building a tower that is one big pyramid. You'll need to plan the shapes carefully to make sure they all fit together. You might want to try to make your tower much taller. Can you make a tower that stands taller than you? The spaghetti pieces bend less if they're shorter—can you make a taller tower by using shorter pieces of spaghetti? If you want your tower to be stable, you'll need to make the base wide and the top the same width or narrower.

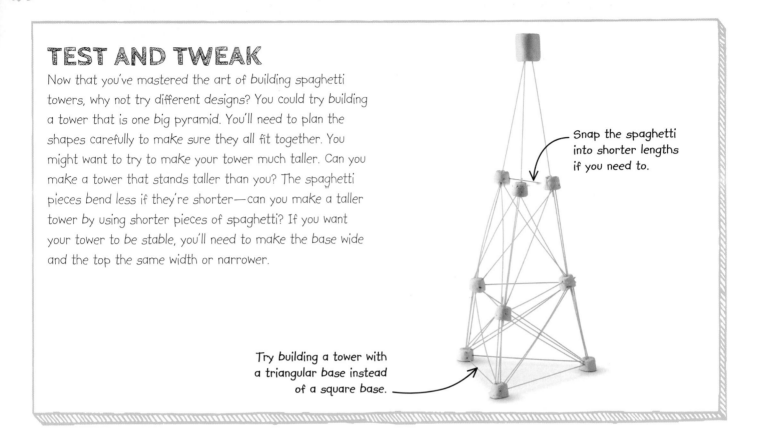

Snap the spaghetti into shorter lengths if you need to.

Try building a tower with a triangular base instead of a square base.

HOW IT WORKS

Triangles are the key to the strength of your tower. Unlike a square, which can lean over and turn into a parallelogram when pushed, a triangle can't change shape, so it remains upright and rigid. The base of your tower must also be wide. All objects have something called a center of gravity. This is the midpoint of an object's mass, where all its mass appears to be concentrated. Objects are stable if the center of gravity is within the base. If an object leans so much that the center of gravity is outside the base, it will fall.

Center of gravity

STABLE   STABLE   STABLE   UNSTABLE

REAL WORLD: ENGINEERING
TOKYO SKYTREE

With a height of 2,080 ft (634 m), the Tokyo Skytree in Japan is the tallest tower in the world. It's made of steel tubes arranged as strong triangles, and its base is much wider than its top.

NEWSPAPER STOOL

A single sheet of newspaper is very flimsy. It crumples and folds easily, and you would probably never think of using it to make anything really strong. But use lots of sheets of newspaper together in just the right way, and you can make a stool so strong that it can support your weight!

Duct tape holds all the rolls together to make the stool.

Individual sheets of newspaper are not very strong at all.

Each roll of newspaper is held together by clear tape.

HOW TO MAKE A
NEWSPAPER STOOL

You'll have to collect lots of newspaper to do this activity. If you want to make your stool really strong, you'll need to roll the newspaper very tightly. You might want to ask a friend to help so that one of you can roll and the other can tape. If you ever want to dismantle your stool, remove the tape first—then you can recycle the newspaper.

Time
45 minutes

Difficulty
Easy

WHAT YOU NEED

Clear tape

Duct tape

Scissors

Lots of newspapers

1 Roll up about 20 sheets of newspaper together lengthwise. Roll it as tightly as you can. The roll should feel strong and rigid.

Try to keep the newspaper rolled as tightly as possible.

2 Wrap clear tape around the roll, close to each end. You might want to ask someone to help you, as you need at least one hand to hold the roll. Repeat until you have 25 rolls.

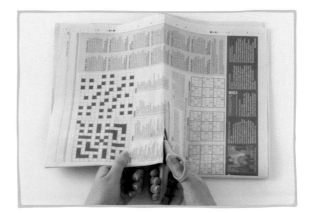

3 Take another pile of about 20 sheets and cut it in half. You will use the two halves to make two short rolls.

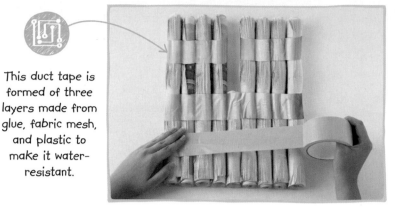

This duct tape is formed of three layers made from glue, fabric mesh, and plastic to make it water-resistant.

4 Roll up and tape each half at the ends as before, so you finish with two rolls half the length of the others.

5 Line up eight long rolls with one short roll in the middle. Wrap duct tape around them to secure them all together. Repeat this step with another eight long rolls and one short roll.

You now have two panels that can interlock with one another.

The rolls of paper are strong in compression: you can sit on the stool.

6 Slot one set of paper rolls into the other, using the gaps left by the short rolls in the middle of each. You should now have an X-shape that stands up on its own.

Make sure the seat is securely attached to the X-shape with lots of tape, to stop it from falling off!

The paper rolls are arranged in a cross, giving the stool stability.

7 To make your seat, line up the remaining nine long rolls of newspaper and secure them together with duct tape. Stand your X-shape on top of your joined rolls and use duct tape to attach it.

8 Stand your stool the right way up, so that the row of nine rolls is on top. Your stool is finished. Now go ahead and sit on it!

HOW IT WORKS

The rolls of paper you used to make the stool are strong in two ways. First, a cylinder has no corners, so no point is weaker than any other, making it a very strong shape. Second, by rolling the paper rolls very tightly, you are increasing the density of the cylinders—packing more matter (stuff) into the same volume (space). If you made the rolls looser so they were much less dense, they wouldn't be as strong.

The force to support your weight comes from the molecules that make up the paper. When you sit on the stool, you squash, or compress, the paper slightly. The molecules of which the paper is made are pushed a tiny bit closer together, and that produces an equal force that pushes in the opposite direction—as if there are springs between them.

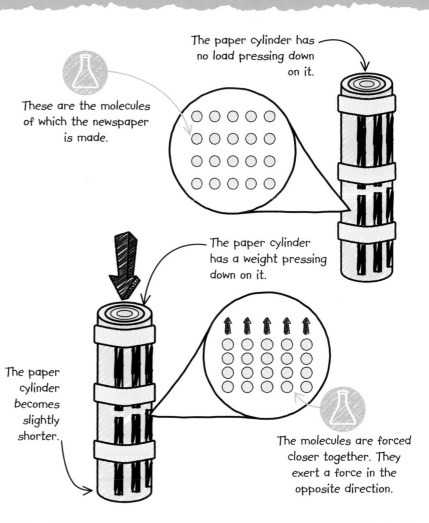

These are the molecules of which the newspaper is made.

The paper cylinder has no load pressing down on it.

The paper cylinder has a weight pressing down on it.

The paper cylinder becomes slightly shorter.

The molecules are forced closer together. They exert a force in the opposite direction.

REAL WORLD: ENGINEERING
COMPRESSED COLUMNS

You can see cylindrical shapes like the paper rolls you used to make your stool in the columns that support big buildings. Just like your paper rolls, these columns are very strong in compression—even stronger than the paper, as they are made of dense stone.

REAL WORLD: SCIENCE
HOLLOW BONES

The long bones in your legs that support your weight work in a similar way to the paper rolls in your stool. They are hollow in the middle (to allow for the marrow, where blood cells are made) but very dense and strong around the outside. The dense part of the bone is made up of many small tubes (osteons), each one very weak. Just as several rolls of paper bound together can support a weight, the clusters of osteons make the bone very strong.

SUSPENSION BRIDGE

Engineers build huge suspension bridges from concrete and steel cables. The concrete towers support the cables, and the cables support the road, which can carry hundreds of cars and trucks at a time. The best way to understand how these forces work together to make a strong and stable structure is to build your own model suspension bridge. In this activity, you can do just that by using bundles of drinking straws instead of concrete and string instead of steel cables.

The towers are made of bundles of drinking straws.

This is called a suspension bridge because the roadway is suspended from cables.

The road is made of corrugated cardboard.

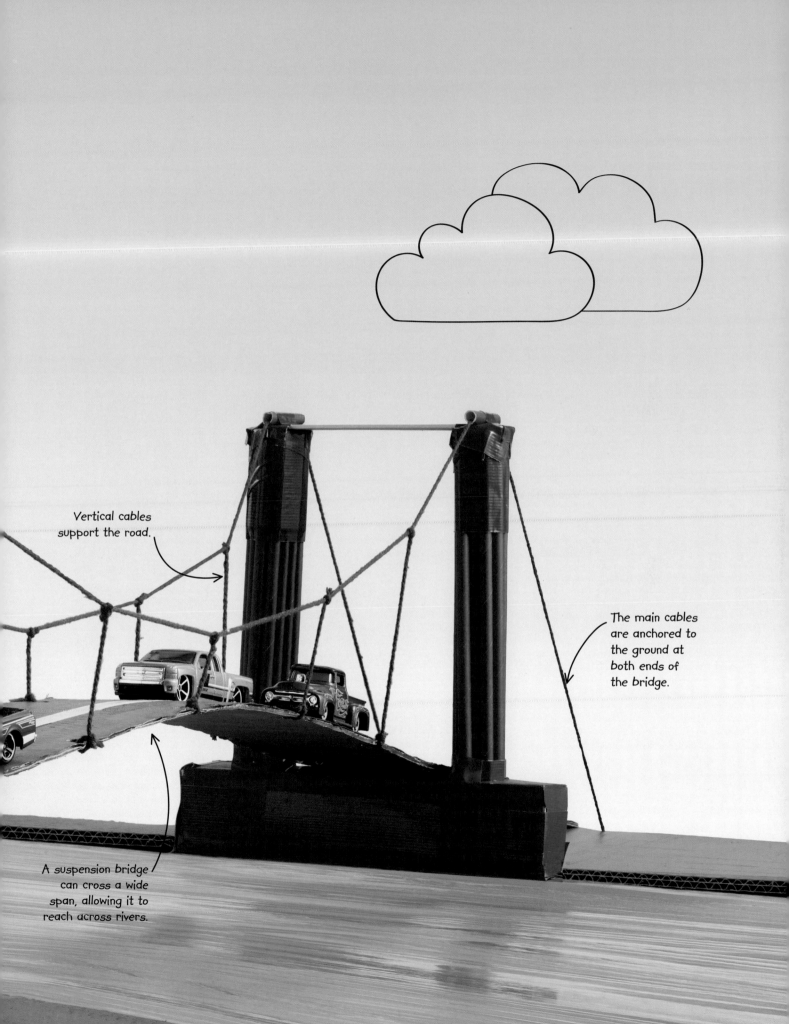

Vertical cables support the road.

The main cables are anchored to the ground at both ends of the bridge.

A suspension bridge can cross a wide span, allowing it to reach across rivers.

HOW TO MAKE A
SUSPENSION BRIDGE

The bases of the bridge's towers are made from toothpaste tube boxes. If you can't find any, you can make boxes the right size from cardboard. The towers are made from bundles of drinking straws. We used 15 in each bundle—if your straws are wider or narrower than ours, use fewer or more straws.

Time
60 minutes

Difficulty
Hard

WHAT YOU NEED

Double-sided tape

Duct tape

String

Rubber band

Hole punch

Scissors

Pencil

Gray paint

Four lollipop sticks

Black felt-tip pen

Paintbrush

White paint

Small pebbles

Ruler

Two toothpaste boxes, each 2 in x 2 in x 8 in (5 cm x 5 cm x 20 cm)

Lots of corrugated cardboard

61 paper straws

Use a rubber band to hold the bundle temporarily before wrapping the tape around.

1 Make a bundle of 15 straws. Now wrap a piece of duct tape around each end. Repeat three times to make a total of four towers.

2 Firmly tape two lollipop sticks side by side across the tops of two of your towers. Repeat with the other two towers.

3 Cut four 1 in (2½ cm) pieces from the last straw. These will hold the bridge's two main cables in place.

The bridge's main cables will pass through these straws.

4 Tape each piece of straw to the top of a tower at a 90-degree angle to the lollipop sticks.

If you like, paint the toothpaste boxes first.

5 Draw around the *bases* of your towers on one side of each toothpaste box. Cut around the lines and push the towers into the holes.

The pebbles are ballast—their weight makes the bridge stable.

6 Fill both boxes with the pebbles. You may need to adjust the position of the towers to fit the pebbles around them. Close the boxes and secure them with duct tape.

7 Cut out two 8 in (20 cm) wide cardboard squares and, if you want, paint the tops gray. These will form the base your bridge stands on.

Make sure the painted side of the base faces upward.

8 When the paint is dry, tape the toothpaste boxes to the bases. Ensure the edge of each box lines up with the edge of the base.

If you like, paint a white line in the center of the road.

9 To make the road, take a piece of cardboard 3¼ ft (1 m) long and as wide as the gap between the towers. Then paint it grey.

10 Add a piece of double-sided tape between the two towers on each base. Remove the protective strip so the tape is sticky.

Tape the road down here.

11 Press the road onto the double-sided tape at both ends, as shown here, and then tape the end of the road to the edge of the base.

12 If you put objects on the bridge now, it will sag. That's because the bridge still needs cables to support heavy weights.

13 Make pen marks 4 in (10 cm) apart along both sides of the road to mark the points where cables will attach.

Take care not to punch holes through the edge of the road.

14 Use a hole punch to make a hole at each mark. Make sure you push the hole punch far enough onto the road that the hole isn't too near the edge.

15 Now make your cables. Cut two long pieces of string, each 5 ft (1½ m) in length. Cut 10 short pieces of string, each 6 in (15 cm) long.

16 Thread the long pieces of string through the short straws on top of both ends of the bridge. You should then have two parallel "cables."

The long pieces of string will be the bridge's main cables. In a real bridge, the cables are made from steel.

17 Cut short slits in the base at both ends of the bridge, then wedge the ends of the main cables into the slits. Don't pull the string tight—it should hang in the middle of the bridge.

Start in the center and work outward.

18 Tie the short pieces of string between the holes in the road and the main cables. Starting from the middle, they should be about 1¼ in (3 cm), 2 in (5 cm), and 2¾ in (7 cm) long.

19 Pull the main cables through the slits in the bases so that they're taut. Secure the ends of the bridge to a table or board with tape. Your suspension bridge is now complete!

20 Try placing objects on the road to see how well the bridge supports their weight. When the bridge is carrying a heavy load, touch the vertical strings and the main cables to see if you can feel them become more taut.

If any of the vertical strings ("hangers") are too loose, untie and shorten them slightly.

Small, heavy objects like toy cars are ideal for testing the stability of your bridge.

HOW IT WORKS

If you put objects on your bridge when it isn't supported by cables, the load will make the road sag. A real bridge without cables would break apart under a heavy load. The bridge must be able to push upward on the load to support it. This upward force is supplied by the tension in the vertical strings—and they are supported at the top by tension in the main cables. The main cables are supported by the towers, which are themselves supported by the ground.

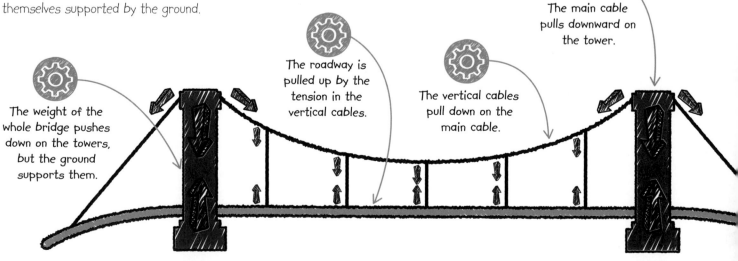

The main cable pulls downward on the tower.

The roadway is pulled up by the tension in the vertical cables.

The vertical cables pull down on the main cable.

The weight of the whole bridge pushes down on the towers, but the ground supports them.

Suspension bridges can achieve a wider span than any other kind of bridge.

The roadway should arch in the middle slightly when the bridge is finished.

The main cables must be firmly anchored at each end of the bridge to maintain their tension.

TEST AND TWEAK

Once you know how to build a model suspension bridge, why not try making a longer, taller, or wider one? Can larger bridges carry just as much weight, or do they need more cables to support them? Do the main cables need to be anchored to the ground, or would the bridge still work if they're only anchored to the road? What's the maximum weight your bridge can support? Load it until it collapses to find out!

REAL WORLD: ENGINEERING
GOLDEN GATE BRIDGE

Perhaps the best-known suspension bridge in the world is the Golden Gate Bridge just north of San Francisco, CA. Around 112,000 vehicles cross this bridge every day. The suspended roadway is 1⅗ miles (2.7 km) long and is held high above the ocean by two main cables measuring 1⅖ miles (2.3 km) long.

REAL WORLD: TECHNOLOGY
CABLE-SUPPORTED ROOF

BC Place sports stadium in Vancouver, Canada, has a fabric roof held up by 22 miles (35 km) of steel cables. The cables are supported by 36 steel towers that do the same job as the towers in a suspension bridge. The fabric roof is strong enough to support 7,700 tons of snow and can retract to create an open-air stadium when the weather is good.

GEODESIC DOME

This impressive structure is known as a geodesic dome. It's easy to make, and though it is quite light and looks fragile, it is actually extremely sturdy because of its shape. Once you've made your dome, you can cover it with clear cellophane to make a small greenhouse.

Triangles make the structure sturdy and stable.

Cellophane traps heat from the Sun inside the greenhouse, making it warmer.

The straws
are the struts.

Succulent plants
can survive in hot
environments with little
rain, such as the inside
of a greenhouse.

Pipe cleaners,
hidden by the tape,
connect the struts.

HOW TO MAKE A
GEODESIC DOME

This geodesic dome is made of 65 struts, of two different lengths, joined together by connectors made from pipe cleaners. We've used two kinds of paper straws to distinguish the long struts from the short struts, as well as two kinds of pipe cleaners: one for the feet connectors at the base of the dome, and one for the regular connectors. You don't have to use the same colors as we have.

Time
60 minutes

Difficulty
Hard

WHAT YOU NEED

Cellophane

Clear sticky tape

Scissors

Pencil

30 paper straws of one colour

Lots of coloured tape

Ruler

35 paper straws of a different colour

Five pipe cleaners of one colour

10 pipe cleaners of a different colour

1 First, make the 35 long struts from straws. They should be 5 in (12 cm) long. For each one, draw a line first, then cut the straw at the line.

2 Now make 30 short struts from the other straws. These should be 4½ in (11 cm) long. Make sure you recycle the bits of straw you don't need from steps 1 and 2.

3 Gather together five pipe cleaners of one color and 10 of the other. Fold each one in half and cut, and then cut each half in half again.

You should end up with 20 of one color and 40 of the other.

4 Twist together pairs of pipe cleaners from the pile of 20, just like in the picture here, to make 10 "feet" for your dome.

5 To make the connectors, twist together three lengths of the other pipe cleaner. You'll need 12 of these connectors altogether.

A flat 10-sided shape is called a decagon.

6 Connect 10 of the long struts by using the pipe cleaner feet. You'll end up with a 10-sided shape.

7 Use the connectors to begin building up the dome, forming the bottom layer of triangles. Alternate the long and the short struts, as shown.

Short strut

Make these short struts nearly vertical, leaning slightly inward.

8 Add short struts around the top of the first layer, then wherever four short struts meet, add another short strut.

Long

Long

Short

9 Around each near-vertical short strut, use a connector to add two long struts, as shown.

The short struts form five triangles inside each pentagon.

10 Connect five more of the long struts around the top of the middle layer. These will form a pentagon on top of the dome.

One strut will have two pipe cleaner legs tucked into it.

11 To complete the top of the dome, join five short struts with a connector. Tuck the spare sixth leg of the connector into one of the struts.

12 Join the five remaining short struts to the spare connectors at the top of the dome.

The cellophane covering will turn your geodesic dome into a small greenhouse ready for plants.

13 Wrap short lengths of colored tape around all the joints to strengthen the structure.

14 Now cover your dome in cellophane and secure the pieces in place with clear tape. Your geodesic dome is complete!

HOW IT WORKS

The geodesic design is very sturdy because it has the stability of the triangle shape as its building block. Triangles are strong because they don't distort when put under pressure. If pressure is put on one corner of a triangle, the other two corners distribute the force evenly. In your geodesic dome, the triangles are repeated, so any force on the building divides repeatedly at each intersection and spreads efficiently through the structure.

In a geodesic dome, the weight of the building is distributed efficiently across the whole structure.

The forces are reduced at each level of the dome.

The triangle shape divides the forces evenly at every intersection.

REAL WORLD: SCIENCE
BUCKMINSTERFULLERENE

In 1986, scientists discovered a form of the element carbon whose atoms are arranged in a geodesic shape of pentagons and hexagons. This form of carbon was named buckminsterfullerene, after one of the most important designers of geodesic domes, the American architect Richard Buckminster Fuller.

PANTOGRAPH

Invented in 1603, the pantograph is a device that was once used to copy drawings and enlarge them at the same time. It's made of four rigid pieces that pivot around joints. When you move the pencil in the middle, the end of the right arm copies the movement of your hand but covers greater distances. The effect is quite spooky, as though an invisible hand is holding the second pen and copying you. Why not try this spooky drawing machine for yourself?

Joints made with paper fasteners allow the pantograph to flex and stretch.

The whole pantograph pivots around this point, which is attached to the table with adhesive putty.

Move this pencil with your hand to draw a picture.

This pen draws an enlarged copy of your picture.

HOW TO MAKE A
PANTOGRAPH

Your pantograph is made of four rectangles of cardboard joined by paper fasteners. It's important that the cardboard can move freely at the joints. The pantograph works best if you draw a simple picture in a single continuous line without lifting the pencil.

Time
30 minutes

Difficulty
Medium

WHAT YOU NEED

Felt-tip pens

Adhesive putty

Clear tape

Pencil

Paintbrush

Two bottle caps

Scissors

Paint

Paper fasteners

Corrugated cardboard

Paper

Ruler

1 Use the pencil to draw three rectangles on the cardboard, each 20 in (50 cm) long by 2 in (5 cm) wide. Cut them out.

8 in

2 Use a pencil to mark a line on one of the rectangles, 8 in (20 cm) from the end. Cut across this line to make two rectangles, one 8 in (20 cm) long and the other 12 in (30 cm).

3 You now have all four pieces for your pantograph. If you like, paint them and allow the paint to dry.

Place adhesive putty underneath and use a sharp pencil to make the holes.

4 On every piece, make pencil marks 1 in (2½ cm) from the ends, halfway from each side. Make holes through the marks using the pencil.

5 Lay the pieces exactly as shown here, with the holes lining up.

Right arm

Left arm

When this rectangle moves on its hinged corners, the opposite sides remain parallel, forming a shape called a parallelogram.

Joints are connections between moving parts in a machine.

Don't fasten this joint yet.

6 Poke paper fasteners through the two holes shown and fold the metal wings back. Don't fasten the other holes yet.

7 Place a bottle cap on a lump of adhesive putty and use a sharp pencil to make a hole in it. Do the same to the other bottle cap.

8 Use a paper fastener to attach a bottle cap to the end of the left arm. Push in a lump of adhesive putty. This will secure the arm to the table.

Use a paper fastener to secure the bottle cap.

9 Attach the other bottle cap underneath the joint between the two arms. This will keep the cardboard parts raised above the table.

10 Wrap tape around the ends of the two short bits of cardboard and the free end of the right arm. This will stop the cardboard splitting when you push the pencil and pen through.

11 Push the pencil through the taped ends of the short bits of cardboard and leave it in place. Make a hole through the end of the long arm and push the felt-tip pen through it.

12 To use the pantograph, draw a picture with the pencil and watch the felt-tip pen as it makes a larger copy. Try to do this in one continuous movement, without lifting the pencil or repeating lines. You can also use the pantograph to trace existing pictures and enlarge them.

The pantograph acts as a lever that magnifies movement rather than forces.

If the pantograph won't stay in place as you use it, hold down the attached end with one hand.

HOW IT WORKS

The pantograph is an example of a mechanical linkage—a machine made of rigid pieces that are joined but can still move. A mechanical linkage changes one kind of movement into another. In this case, the movement you put in is magnified. In the center of the pantograph is a parallelogram—a shape whose opposite sides are parallel (lined up in the same direction). The pencil and pen are mounted on parallel parts, so they trace out the same shape as they move. However, because the pen is on a longer arm, the shape it draws is magnified. The magnification equals the length of the pen's arm divided by the length of the pencil's arm (A ÷ B in the diagram).

Large movement of felt-tip pen

Small movement of pencil

A

B

Fixed point

Increasing the length of the long arm increases the scale by which pictures are enlarged.

Make sure the piece of paper is big enough for the enlarged picture.

The pantograph can't press the felt-tip down, so make sure the ink flows easily.

You can use a pantograph to shrink pictures by swapping which pen you hold.

REAL WORLD: SCIENCE
UMBRELLA

Mechanical linkages are found in many different machines and devices, including something you probably have at home: an umbrella. When you push up on the sliding part inside an umbrella (the rider), the rods and pivots inside the umbrella magnify the movement of your hand to lift up the entire canopy, giving you shelter from the rain.

STURDY SANDCASTLE

If you've ever made a sandcastle, you'll know you have to use a bit of water to make the sand damp in order to bind the grains together. Try it with dry sand and you'll end up with a heap because there's nothing to stick the grains together. But even a castle made with damp sand will collapse under a little weight. With the help of a little science and engineering, however, this project reveals how you can make a super-strong sandcastle—one that might even be able to support your weight!

In wet sand, the water binds the sand grains, helping to hold the structure together.

There is a force caused by the books pressing downward on the sandcastle.

The sandcastle is "reinforced," which means it has been strengthened with extra material.

Layers of gauze give this castle extra strength.

HOW TO BUILD A
STURDY
SANDCASTLE

There is a special ingredient that makes this sandcastle strong: strips of gauze. Apart from that, it's just like most sandcastles—you fill a bucket with damp sand, then turn it over. If you do this activity on a beach, make sure you take the gauze strips with you afterward and dispose of them carefully. You can leave the sand behind though!

Time
15 minutes

Difficulty
Easy

WHAT YOU NEED

Water

Trowel

Gauze

Scissors

Bucket

Sand

Heavy books

1 Pour enough water into the sand to make the sand slightly damp. Stir the mixture thoroughly, so that there is no dry sand and no excess water.

2 Use the trowel to make a layer of sand about 2 in (5 cm) deep in the bottom of the bucket. Spread the sand evenly across the bucket's base.

3 Press down firmly on the damp sand with your hand to compact it. Make sure the layer is flat.

As you start to build your sandcastle and press down, you force the sand grains together.

4 Carefully cut several strips of gauze that are about as long as your bucket is wide. You can always cut more if you run out of pieces.

The number of layers depends on the size of your bucket.

Gauze is thin but strong. It is made of a fine mesh of woven fabric.

5 Put a few strips of gauze on top of the layer of sand. Place them so that they overlap slightly, in order to cover the sand completely.

6 Keep adding layers of damp sand 2 in (5 cm) deep with strips of gauze between them. Press down each layer firmly.

7 Don't worry too much if your bucket is an odd shape, like this one. Just cover as much of each sand layer as possible.

8 Fill the bucket to the top with sand. Cover this final layer with strips of gauze that extend slightly over the edge of the bucket.

Lift up your bucket slowly!

9 With one hand over the gauze strips to stop them from falling off, carefully turn the bucket upside down and place it on the ground or a table.

10 Gently tap the sides of the bucket, and then lift it away, just as you would if you were making an ordinary sandcastle.

11 Your sandcastle is ready to test! To see how sturdy it is, gently place one of the heavy books on top.

12 Load more books on top of your sandcastle. See how heavy a load your sandcastle can support before it collapses!

Place the books carefully on top of your sandcastle!

Engineers use the word "loading" to describe the forces a structure has to withstand.

This is what happens to a normal sandcastle when you put books on it!

TEST AND TWEAK

Your sandcastle should be able to support quite a heavy load, but can you make it even stronger? What happens if you replace the strips of gauze with paper, plastic bags, or parts of an old T-shirt? Does coarse or gritty sand make a better sandcastle than fine sand? Could you make a castle from gravel instead of sand?

HOW IT WORKS

Sand grains are made of rock and shells that have been broken down into tiny pieces by the action of moving water in the ocean or in rivers. An ordinary sandcastle would collapse if you placed a load on top of it, because the sand grains can easily slip sideways over each other. But your sandcastle can support a load because the gauze strips increase the friction between the grains as they slip sideways. Friction is the resistance created when two or more objects are pushing past each other. Increasing the friction between the gauze and the grains prevents the grains from slipping sideways.

With reinforcement, the sandcastle is able to support a heavy load.

The heavy load pushes the sand grains together.

Without reinforcement, there is little friction, or resistance. The sand grains slip sideways, collapsing into a pile.

ORDINARY SANDCASTLE

REINFORCED SANDCASTLE

The strips of gauze increase the amount of friction in the structure, so the sand grains can't slide sideways as easily.

REAL WORLD: ENGINEERING
STABILIZING SLOPES

The combination of sand and strips of gauze used to build your sandcastle is similar to a technique used by engineers to create reinforced structures. They use grainy materials like soil or sand and pack them between strips of mesh. Where a motorway carves through the land, engineers use this technique to reinforce unstable slopes beside the road. Seawalls protecting coastal areas are also built in this way, as they are able to absorb the impact of waves and prevent coastal erosion.

LIGHT AND SOUND

Waves are associated with water, but some types of energy, such as light and sound, also travel in waves. In this chapter, you'll learn all about waves by making your own wave machine. You'll also study light with a scientific device called a spectroscope. The sounds we hear are made by waves of vibrations that disturb the air. You'll make musical sounds by creating your own harmonica and guitar, as well as hear the sound of bells—with spoons!

The modeling clay balls swing back and forth as the wave's energy travels through the machine.

Energy is transferred along the tape.

When you twist the end of the wave machine, you create a wave.

The double layer of tape is strong but flexible enough to twist.

The tape and the skewers twist all the way along the machine (and back again).

TRANSFERRING ENERGY

WAVE MACHINE

Throw a stone in a pond and it makes waves. It might look like circles of water are rushing outward, but in fact the water is only moving up and down as energy transfers through it. Waves transfer energy from place to place, which makes them very useful. We can use them to send and receive information, to heat up food, and to surf! This twisting wave machine lets you see waves in action.

HOW TO MAKE A
WAVE MACHINE

You'll make your wave machine from duct tape and wooden skewers. The tape is very sticky and can easily become stuck to itself, so take your time. The skewers have a sharp point at one end, so be careful. You'll need to work somewhere with plenty of space because your wave machine will be about 9 ft (3 m) long!

Time
30 minutes

Difficulty
Easy

WHAT YOU NEED

Scissors

Measuring tape

Duct tape

Wooden skewers

Modeling clay

1 First, you'll make the handles. Carefully cut a length of tape about twice as long as a skewer. Lay it down on the table sticky side up.

2 Put 10 skewers onto the tape's center. Roll the tape tightly around the skewers and fold the ends over, then repeat to make another handle.

3 Pull out some of the tape, with the sticky side facing upward. Place one handle onto the tape and roll it forward a short way to secure it.

4 Roll out about 3 ft (1 m) of tape. Working from the end nearest the handle, place a skewer across the tape every 2 in (5 cm) or so.

5 Roll out another 3 ft (1 m) of tape and keep adding a skewer every 2 in (5 cm). Repeat this step so your wave machine is about 9 ft (3 m) long.

Leave about 4 in (10 cm) between the last skewer and the handle.

6 When the wave machine is 9 ft (3 m) long, roll out another 8 in (20 cm) of tape and cut. Place the other handle on top of the tape and roll it for 4 in (10 cm), leaving a 4 in (10 cm) gap without skewers.

7 Starting at the second handle, place a new strip of tape sticky side down onto the skewers, on top of and all the way along the upturned tape.

8 Now roll lots of small round balls of modeling clay of a similar size—two for each wooden skewer you've placed on the tape.

9 Push one ball of modeling clay onto each end of every skewer. Be careful not to stab your fingers on the sharp ends of the skewers.

10 Your wave machine is ready to use! Ask a friend to hold one handle completely still, or secure the handle to a piece of furniture. Hold the other handle, stretching it out gently. Now twist it by alternately lifting your left and right hand.

TEST AND TWEAK

Can you make different waves by changing the design of your wave machine? You could try moving the wooden skewers closer together or farther apart and making the modeling clay balls smaller or larger—or try taking some of them off altogether! You could also work out the speed of your waves in feet or meters per second by measuring the tape, timing how long a wave takes to travel along it, and dividing the distance by the time.

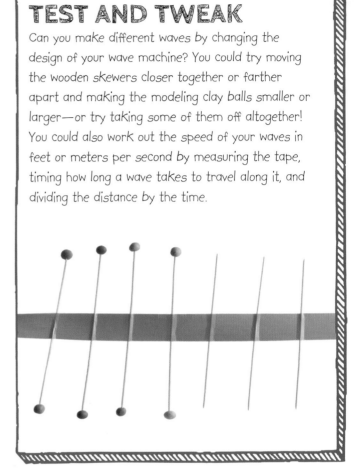

The energy you use twisting the handle is transferred along your wave machine.

HOW IT WORKS

Waves are all around us and take many different forms, from ripples in water to sound waves, light, and radio waves. Your wave machine shows how waves transfer energy from place to place. When you twist the handle, the energy you use transfers along the wave machine. Only the energy moves forward—the modeling clay balls merely wobble back and forth as they pass on the energy. All types of waves have a speed, a wavelength, and a frequency. The speed is how fast the wave travels. The wavelength is the distance between two "peaks" or "troughs." The frequency is how many waves pass a particular point every second.

REAL WORLD: TECHNOLOGY
FIBER-OPTIC CABLES

Much of the information on the internet is shared around the world at high speed by waves of infrared radiation. These light waves pass through thin glass threads known as optical fibers. The light waves reflect and bounce off the insides of the glass threads, traveling along without losing much of their energy and transmitting data over huge distances.

LOW FREQUENCY

Wavelength

0   1

A peak is where the end of a skewer is at its highest point.

A trough is where the end of a skewer is at its lowest.

HIGH FREQUENCY

Wavelength

0   1

The amplitude is the distance between the peak and midpoint of a wave.

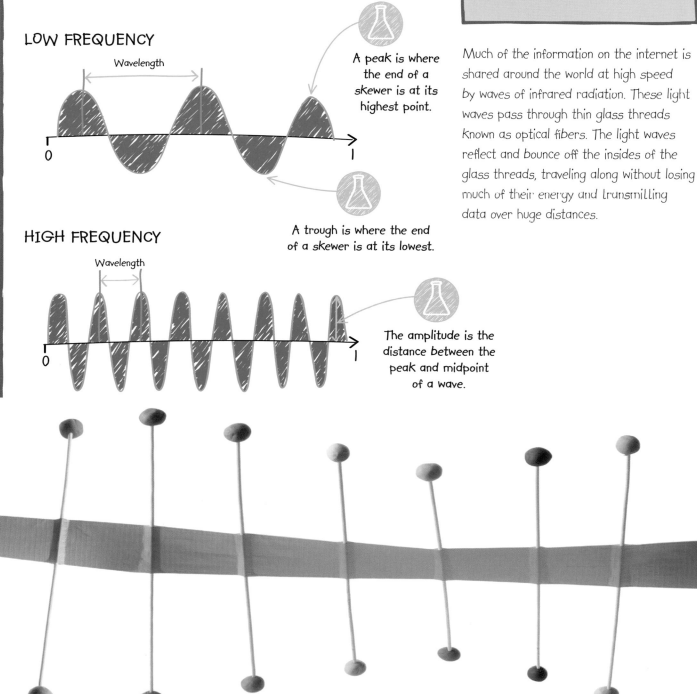

Light from a flashlight appears white, but it is a mix of different colors. It enters through a slit at the top of the spectroscope.

Daylight is a good source of white light if you don't have a flashlight available.

When white light hits the shiny side of the CD, it bounces off and separates into different colors.

A viewing window lets you see and study the spectrum, or range, of colors present in the light.

SPLITTING LIGHT

SPECTROSCOPE

It might look white, but light is actually a mix of different colors. You can see these colors in a rainbow, because each color bends at a different angle as it bounces off raindrops. Scientists use a device known as a spectroscope to study the range of colors (the spectrum) in different kinds of light. In this activity, you can make your own spectroscope.

HOW TO BUILD A
SPECTROSCOPE

In order to clearly *see* the spectrum of colors that make up white light, you'll need a shiny CD for the light to bounce off. A slit at the top of a dark tube lets a small amount of light into the tube and onto the CD. You'll need to use a protractor to measure the angle at which you place the CD. You'll also need black electrical tape to block out unwanted light.

Time
30 minutes

Difficulty
Medium

WHAT YOU NEED

Protractor

Black electrical tape

Paint

Scissors

Flashlight

Paintbrush

Pencil

Black cardstock

Old CD

Cardboard tube

Ruler

1 Using the pencil, make a mark 1¼ in (3 cm) from one end of the cardboard tube.

1¼ in (3 cm)

2 Wrap the black cardstock around the cardboard tube at the mark. Use it as a guide to draw a line around the tube.

3 Hold the protractor on the tube so the protractor's zero line runs along the pencil line. Draw a short line angled at 30 degrees.

Check that the straight edge of your protractor is still lined up with the pencil line you drew.

4 Move the protractor and draw another line, angled at 30 degrees in the other direction, so the two slanted lines almost meet.

5 Using the ruler, extend both slanted lines so they meet the line that goes around the cardboard tube, forming a triangle.

6 On the opposite side of the tube from the triangle, draw a rectangle ¾ in (2 cm) high and ½ in (1 cm) wide above the pencil line.

Pinch the tube at the bottom to pop the slit open.

7 Cut along the two slanted lines so that you end up with an angled slot. This is where you'll slide in your old CD.

8 Now carefully cut out the small rectangle you drew to make a viewing window for your spectroscope. Ask an adult to help if you get stuck.

9 Paint the cardboard tube in any color or design you like, then leave the paint to dry.

10 Push the CD into the angled slot, with the shiny, bottom surface facing upward.

It's crucial to get the angle of the CD just right so you can see the spectrum clearly.

11 Secure the CD in place inside the slot using *black electrical tape*.

12 Use strips of electrical tape to close off the end of the cardboard tube closest to the CD. Make sure no light can get into the tube.

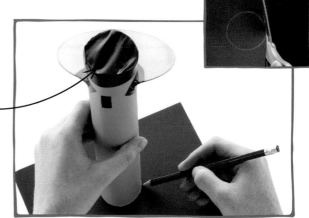

The end closest to the CD should be completely covered with black electrical tape.

13 Draw around the open end of the cardboard tube onto the *black piece of card* using a pencil. Carefully cut out the circle.

14 The circle of card will cover the open end of the tube, but it needs a slit to let in light. To make the slit, first fold the circle in half.

15 Carefully cut two lines close together at right angles from the middle of the fold. Cut off the thin piece between the lines.

16 Unfold the circle and tape it over the open end of the tube. The slit should run from side to side, not front to back, so that it aligns with the slot holding the CD.

Light from the flashlight enters the slit in the top of the spectroscope.

The light hits the shiny CD and bounces off, splitting into different colors.

Carefully tape around the circle of black card to hold it in place.

17 Your spectroscope is now ready to use! Shine a flashlight into the top and look through the viewing window to see the spectrum. You could also try other light sources, such as daylight through a window, but don't point your spectroscope directly at the Sun.

HOW IT WORKS

White light is a mixture of all the colors of the rainbow. When it hits a reflective object, all these colors bounce off, or reflect. Light hitting the shiny underside of a CD reflects in a different way. All the colors reflect, but each one bounces off in a different direction. The different colors spread out to form a spectrum.

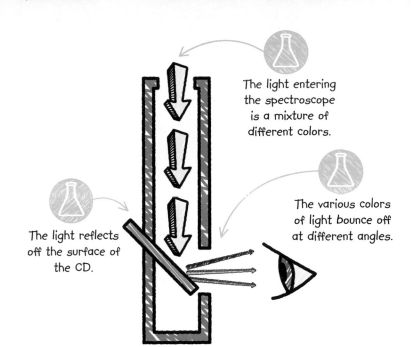

The light entering the spectroscope is a mixture of different colors.

The light reflects off the surface of the CD.

The various colors of light bounce off at different angles.

COMPARING DIFFERENT LIGHT SOURCES

If you compare different light sources, such as daylight or the screen of a cell phone, you'll find that each one produces a distinctive spectrum. Daylight produces a continuous spectrum, with every color of the rainbow and no gaps. In contrast, an artificial light source typically produces only certain colors, so its spectrum has colored lines with black gaps between them.

The light from the Sun produces a continuous spectrum.

DAYLIGHT

A phone screen produces only red, green, and blue light, so its spectrum looks different.

CELL PHONE

REAL WORLD: SCIENCE
THE LIGHT OF STARS

Each of the chemical elements of which matter is made produces light with a different spectrum when it burns. Chemists in laboratories can identify which elements are present in different substances by using spectroscopes to study the light they give off when burned. Astronomers also use spectroscopes to study light from stars; from lines in the spectrum, they can tell which elements are present.

SINGING SPOONS

In this activity, you'll use metal spoons to create amazing noises that sound like bells or gongs chiming—but you'll only hear these incredible sounds if you put your fingers in your ears! When the spoons swing and bang together, the metal flexes a tiny amount, and then flexes back again repeatedly. These movements, known as vibrations, are too fast and small to see, but they cause the string attached to the spoon to vibrate as well. The vibrations pass along the string and ultimately into your ears!

You'll need to place your fingers gently into your ears to hear the sounds!

Vibrations pass along the string and through your fingers.

Hanging the spoons from a string means they are able to vibrate freely.

The spoons clink as they knock together, but when you put your fingers in your ears, they sound different.

HOW TO MAKE SINGING SPOONS

To hear the amazing sounds that spoons can produce, all you need to do is secure three metal spoons to a string, wrap the string around your fingers, put your fingers in your ears, and knock the spoons together. This activity is super simple and quick to do, but you'll be surprised by the results!

Time
10 minutes

Difficulty
Easy

WHAT YOU NEED

String

Duct tape

Scissors

Three metal spoons

This string will carry the vibrations made by the spoons as they knock together.

1 Cut a piece of string that is about twice the length of your arm. Lay it flat on a table.

Make sure you press the tape down firmly.

2 At the string's middle point, place the ends of the spoons about an inch apart. Secure each spoon to the string with a thin piece of duct tape.

When a material like metal vibrates, it produces sound. Metal makes a different noise from other materials, such as plastic or wood.

3 Dangle the spoons in front of you and wrap the string around one finger of each hand. Knock the spoons together—they'll make a sharp, tinny sound.

Putting your fingers in your ears blocks out other noises, so the sound of the spoons seems even louder.

4 Put the fingers with string around them in your ears. Shake the spoons so they knock against each other. The spoons will sound louder and richer, like bells chiming.

TEST AND TWEAK
If you switch the metal spoons for other metal objects, such as keys or nuts and bolts, how does the sound change? Does the experiment still work if you use wooden or plastic spoons instead?

HOW IT WORKS
When metal spoons knock together, they vibrate (move rapidly back and forth). This makes sound because the vibrations make air molecules vibrate, too, creating invisible waves that travel through the air to your ears. Sound waves spread out as they travel through air, so the sound you hear is tinny. But when you put your fingers in your ears, the vibrations pass through solid materials (the string, your fingers, and your skull, which houses your inner ears). Sound waves travel more effectively through solids than air because the molecules are more tightly packed together. As a result, you hear a richer, more complex pattern of sound waves.

The vibrations travel along the string.

The spoon vibrates (flexes back and forth very rapidly).

The spoon's vibration makes air molecules vibrate, too, producing sound waves that spread through the air.

REAL WORLD: TECHNOLOGY
STETHOSCOPE

You can't normally hear your heartbeat, as it's too quiet. However, a doctor can hear it with a device called a stethoscope. At one end is a cup that the doctor presses on your chest to collect the faint sound of the heart beating. A hollow tube channels this sound to the doctor's ears, preventing the sound waves from spreading out in all directions and becoming too faint to hear.

HARMONICA

Here's a fun and simple way to make some musical notes and to learn a bit about the science of sound. Just like a real harmonica, this one has a part that vibrates when you direct air past it with your breath. In this homemade version, it's a piece of paper held between two toothpicks sandwiched between two lollipop sticks. Go on, see what weird and wonderful sounds you can make!

The pitch of the note your harmonica produces—how high or low it is—depends on how fast the paper vibrates. The faster it vibrates, the higher the pitch.

Making harmonicas is a good way to recycle your lollipop sticks, but make sure they are dry first.

As you play the harmonica, you'll be able to feel the tickle of the vibrations that create the sound!

HOW TO MAKE A
HARMONICA

This harmonica is made with lollipop sticks. As you are going to be touching these with your mouth, make sure they are clean. The only other things you need are rubber bands, toothpicks, and a strip of paper. You'll be making music in just a few minutes!

Time
15 minutes

Difficulty
Easy

WHAT YOU NEED

Two rubber bands

Two toothpicks

Pencil

Scissors

Colored paper

Two lollipop sticks

1 On the paper, draw around a lollipop stick with the pencil, then carefully cut around the shape with the scissors.

Sound is produced by vibrating objects that disturb the air around them. In your harmonica, it is the paper that vibrates.

2 Place the piece of paper you cut out on top of one of the lollipop sticks, then place the other lollipop stick on top.

3 Wrap a rubber band several times around one end of the two lollipop sticks so that it holds them together.

4 Wedge a toothpick between the lollipop sticks and slide it as far toward the end with the rubber band as you can.

You should end up with a toothpick wedged in at each end of the harmonica.

5 Wrap another rubber band around the other end of the lollipop sticks, then wedge another toothpick in at that end.

6 Using scissors, carefully trim the toothpicks and discard the extra pieces. Make sure the paper is flat, not crumpled, then hold the harmonica firmly between your lips and blow. Try sucking, too.

What happens when you press the lollipop sticks together with your teeth?

HOW IT WORKS

The toothpick pieces hold the paper firmly at each end. When you blow or suck, air rushing past the paper makes it vibrate, and the vibrations create disturbances in the air that travel outward in all directions as sound waves. If you blow harder or pinch the sticks as you blow, the paper vibrates faster. This creates a higher-pitched sound.

The paper vibrates, making the lollipop sticks vibrate.

The vibrating sticks disturb the air, creating sound waves that move outward.

REAL WORLD: SCIENCE
VIBRATING REEDS

Real harmonicas work in a similar way to your lollipop harmonica. Instead of paper, they have metal sheets called reeds that vibrate when the player blows or sucks through a set of holes. There is at least one reed behind each hole, and each reed is tuned to a different note.

As the buzzer flies, the rubber band makes a sound like a bee.

Swing the string around to make the buzzer fly.

AEROELASTIC FLUTTER
BUZZER

When you whirl this buzzer around, it'll make a sound like a bumblebee. A bee makes a buzz by flapping its wings 200 times a second when it flies. Instead of wings or muscles, your buzzer will use a simple rubber band to mimic a flying bee. The rubber band twists back and forth rapidly as you whirl it through the air, and this fluttering movement creates sound waves.

HOW TO MAKE A
BUZZER

The buzzer is made from a lollipop stick, a rubber band, some cardstock and string, and some adhesive putty. It's quick and easy to make—but you may have to adjust certain things to make your buzzer work well. In particular, you might have to try a few different sizes of rubber bands.

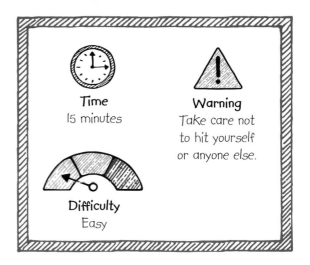

Time
15 minutes

Warning
Take care not to hit yourself or anyone else.

Difficulty
Easy

WHAT YOU NEED

Scissors

String

Pencil

Lollipop stick

Stapler with staples

Adhesive putty

Rubber band

Colored cardstock

Ruler

1 Fold the cardstock in half. Make a tight crease by pressing down firmly along the fold.

Folded edge

2 Lay the lollipop stick next to the folded edge. Make two pencil marks on the fold, each about ½ in (1 cm) from the end of the stick.

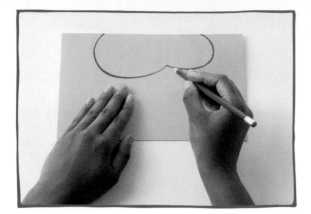

3 Draw a curve between the two pencil marks, like the shape shown here. This will form the outline of the bee's body.

4 Cut along the pencil line. If you open up the folded piece of card, you'll have a bee shape that's symmetrical.

5 Place the lollipop stick inside the fold and staple through the card and the stick twice to hold the stick firmly in place.

6 Cut a length of string at least 20 in (50 cm) long and tie one end securely to one end of the lollipop stick.

7 Secure a lump of adhesive putty at each end of the lollipop stick. Make sure you press it down firmly.

Make sure the adhesive putty is firmly stuck to the lollipop stick.

If you want, draw black stripes and eyes on the card to make the buzzer look beelike.

The elastic band should be taut enough that it doesn't fall off.

8 Stretch the rubber band over the adhesive putty lumps. Check that the band isn't twisted and its sides are parallel to but not touching the lollipop stick.

The folded card creates a streamlined shape that keeps the buzzer facing in one direction as it flies.

If your buzzer loses its buzz after a few minutes, loosen the rubber band from the adhesive putty and try again.

9 Open out the wings slightly. Find an open space where your buzzer won't hit any objects or people and whirl it around in large circular movements as fast as you can. If the buzz is too quiet, experiment with thick and thin rubber bands until you find the one that makes the loudest buzz.

As you whirl the buzzer, the string pulls taut. The pulling force is called centripetal force and keeps the buzzer from flying off in a straight line.

HOW IT WORKS

The buzzing sound is caused by something called aeroelastic flutter. This happens when a flexible object is in fast-moving air, and the air makes it flex back and forth quickly. The rubber band flexes about 200 times a second, which is the same frequency as a bee's wings, so it makes a similar sound. You can create an even louder sound from flutter by sandwiching a blade of grass between the sides of your thumbs and blowing through the gap between them.

Whirling the buzzer in circles causes air to rush quickly over the rubber band.

REAL WORLD: SCIENCE
TACOMA NARROWS BRIDGE

In 1940, the world's third-largest suspension bridge (the Tacoma Narrows Bridge in the US) was hit by strong winds and began to flutter. It twisted back and forth with such violence that it tore itself apart and collapsed. Today, engineers go to great lengths to prevent aeroelastic flutter in structures affected by fast-moving air, such as aircraft and bridges.

The strings are
held in tension.

You can adjust how
tightly the strings are
held by turning the
hooks at the head.

GUITAR

Making music can be a great way to explore the science of sound—and this guitar can help you do both. With fishing line for strings and an ice cream tub for a body, it's easy to make. And if you set it up right, it will make a surprisingly melodious sound. In fact, you'll find this project really hits the right notes!

The vibrations of the strings are passed on to the body of the guitar.

The vibrating body of the guitar disturbs the air, sending out sound waves into the air around it.

HOW TO MAKE A
GUITAR

The two most important features of your guitar are the strings and the body. In this project, the strings are made of fishing line, the body is made of a plastic ice cream tub, and the neck is made of corrugated cardboard.

Time
90 minutes

Difficulty
Hard

WHAT YOU NEED

Scissors

Paint

Paintbrush

Felt-tip pen

Duct tape

Adhesive putty

Large binder clip

Glue

Pencil

Ice cream tub
7½ in × 6 in
(19 cm × 15 cm)

Medium-weight fishing line

Corrugated cardboard
18 in × 14 in
(45 cm × 35 cm)

Eight screw hooks

Ruler

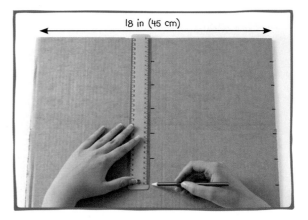

18 in (45 cm)

1 Make pencil marks every 2 in (5 cm) down the shorter side of the cardboard. Repeat the marks in the middle.

2 Using the ruler, draw straight lines that join the marks you made and extend them across the whole width of the cardboard.

3 Cut along the lines so that you end up with seven long rectangles of cardboard, each 18 in (45 cm) long and 2 in (5 cm) wide.

4 On one of the long rectangles, make a pencil mark 9 in (22½ cm) from one end—halfway along its length.

5 Divide the long rectangle into two equal pieces by cutting where you made the pencil mark.

Stacking and gluing the pieces together like this increases the strength of the neck.

6 Stick the other six long rectangles together by applying glue between them and putting them together into a stack.

7 Now glue the two shorter pieces on top of one end of the stack, so that the stack is thicker at one end. This is the neck of the guitar.

8 Mix some glue into the paint. This will thicken it and add strength to the neck when applied to it.

The neck of a guitar has to be strong enough to withstand the stress of the tight strings against it.

9 Apply the glue-and-paint mixture all over your guitar's neck, then leave it for half an hour or so to dry and set.

To make it look like a real guitar, we've decorated ours with painted frets. Frets are metal strips on the neck that help the player find the notes.

This is to ensure that the neck will line up with the side of the tub.

10 Apply a few pieces of duct tape around both ends of the guitar's neck to strengthen them further.

11 Stand the tub on one of its shorter sides. Hold the thick end of the neck against the rim of the tub. Make a mark on the tub next to the thinner part of the neck.

Try to position the neck in the middle of the tub's side.

Put adhesive putty under the tub to protect the table.

12 Hold the thin end of the neck against the end of the tub and line up the top of it with the mark you made. Draw around the neck.

13 Repeat steps 11 and 12 at the other end of the tub. Now carefully use the scissors to make a hole in the middle of each rectangle, from the inside of the box outward.

Take care, as the edges of the pieces will be sharp.

14 Neatly cut out each rectangle, starting at the hole you made. Cut straight lines out to the corners first, then along the rectangle's sides.

If the neck doesn't fit, you might need to make the hole a bit bigger.

15 Push the thin end of the neck through the two holes, until the thick part of the neck juts up against the side of the tub.

Make two of the holes closer to the end than the other two.

16 Line up a ruler at the thick end of the neck. Mark dots at ½ in (1 cm) intervals, making two of them closer to the end, as shown.

17 Screw the four hooks into each of the holes. These will hold the guitar's strings.

18 Draw four more dots on the tape at the thin end of the neck. Make these ½ in (1 cm) apart, too, but all in a line this time.

19 Screw a hook into each of the four dots you drew. In each case, make sure the open part of the hook faces away from the body of the guitar.

20 Cut four pieces of fishing line 4 in (10 cm) longer than the distance from one set of hooks to the other set of hooks.

Make sure the strings don't cross or touch one another.

21 At the thick end of the neck, attach each length of fishing line to a hook. Tie a double knot as tightly as you can.

22 Pull the free end of each length taut and wrap it once or twice around a hook at the other end. Do not tie the line at this end.

23 Pull the ends of the four lengths of fishing line together, keeping them taut, and then secure them with the binder clip. See what happens when you move your fingers up and down the guitar neck while plucking the strings at the same time.

Press down on one or more strings with the fingers of one hand.

Pluck one or more strings with the thumb or fingers of your other hand.

The body of the guitar is what amplifies the sound.

Tighten the strings by turning the hooks at this end until they are taut.

There should be a gap between the strings and the rim of the tub.

You can trim the ends of the strings, but don't make them too short.

HOW IT WORKS

Plucking a string on your guitar causes the string to vibrate many times per second. The more tension there is in the string (the more tightly it's pulled), the more rapidly it vibrates—and the higher the pitch. Pressing a string also raises the pitch. When you press a string, it touches the guitar body in the middle and only its lower half vibrates. This produces a note one octave higher. The strings cause the body of the guitar to vibrate, which disturbs much more air, because it has a larger surface area. This amplifies the vibration of the strings, making it louder.

Plucking the string causes it to vibrate.

Pressing the strings down with your fingers on the cardboard changes the length of the string, which changes the note.

Without the body of the guitar, the sound waves created by the string's vibrations would barely be audible.

The length, tension, and thickness of the string all affect the note produced.

As the body of the guitar vibrates, it amplifies the sound of the strings.

REAL WORLD: TECHNOLOGY
ACOUSTIC GUITAR

Acoustic guitars have six strings, with each one being a different thickness. The thicker the string, the lower the note it makes. This allows a guitar to produce a great range of notes and sounds. Also, unlike your ice cream tub guitar, acoustic guitars have a closed front part with a sound hole, which helps to amplify deeper sounds, as the air inside the guitar is compressed and expands. Finally, the material the guitar is made from greatly affects the sound, as certain materials produce different kinds of sound. Though wood is the most common material, acoustic guitars can also be made from metal or plastic.

GLOSSARY

ACID

A substance that has a pH of less than 7. Strong acids (with pH between 1 and 3) can burn your skin. Weak acids (with pH between 4 and 7) are present in vinegar, lemon juice, and cola.

AERODYNAMICS

The study of how air moves around objects and how the air produces forces such as air resistance and lift.

AIR RESISTANCE

A force that slows down moving objects as they travel through air.

ATMOSPHERIC PRESSURE

The pressure of the air around you, also known as air pressure.

ATOM

A tiny particle of matter. An atom is the smallest part of an element that can exist.

BASE

A substance that has a pH of more than 7. A base is the chemical opposite of an acid.

BEARING

Part of a machine that reduces friction between moving parts. There are bearings in wheels, for example, that allow the wheel to spin freely.

CAM

A machine part that turns rotation into back-and-forth or up-and-down motion.

CARBON DIOXIDE

A chemical compound found as a gas in the atmosphere and in carbonated drinks.

CHEMICAL

A substance that is the same all the way through—it is not a mixture. Chemicals can be elements or compounds, and may be liquids, solids, or gases.

CHEMICAL REACTION

A process in which the atoms of two or more chemicals interact to make new chemicals.

COMPOUND

A chemical made of two or more elements. Water is a compound made of the elements hydrogen and oxygen.

COMPRESSION

A squashing force; the opposite of tension.

CONDUCTION

The flow of heat or electricity through a material.

CONDUCTOR

A material through which heat or electricity flows easily. Metals are good conductors.

CRANK

A machine part that can turn rotation into back-and-forth motion or do the opposite.

CYLINDER

A three-dimensional shape that has a circle as its cross-section.

DENSITY

A measure of how much mass is present in a certain volume of a substance.

ELECTRON

A negatively charged particle found in atoms. Electricity is a flow of electrons.

ELEMENT

A substance made of just one type of atom that cannot be broken down into a simpler substance by chemical reactions.

ELLIPSE

An oval, or flattened circle. The orbits of planets around the Sun are elliptical.

ENERGY

The ability to make things happen. Energy can take various forms, such as electrical energy, kinetic energy (the energy of moving objects), and potential energy (stored energy).

EVAPORATION

The process by which a liquid turns into a gas.

FLUTTER

An energetic vibration created as an object moves through the air (or as air moves past it). The forces exerted by the air cause the object to turn one way, then the other.

FORCE

A push or a pull. Forces change how an object moves by causing it to start or stop moving, speed up or slow down, or change direction. Forces can also change the shape of an object.

FRICTION

A force between surfaces that are in contact. Friction between a tire and the ground pushes a bicycle along as the wheels turn.

GEL

A mixture in which tiny drops of liquid are held in a solid. Jelly is a gel. A gelling agent is a substance that is added to water to turn it into a gel.

GENERATOR

A device that produces electricity when it spins around.

GRAVITY

A force that pulls objects together. Earth's gravity pulls things toward the ground.

HYDROGEN ION

A hydrogen atom that has either lost or gained an electron. The more hydrogen ions in a solution, the lower the solution's pH. Acids release lots of hydrogen ions when they dissolve in water, and bases gain them.

INSULATOR

A material through which heat passes slowly. Your clothes insulate you, slowing down the loss of your body heat to the air around you.

ION

An atom that has a negative or positive electric charge.

LEVER

A rigid bar that modifies force or motion when it swings around a fixed point known as a pivot.

LIFT

An upward force on an object moving through the air. It is the result of the air pressure being greater beneath the object than it is above.

MASS

A measure of the amount of matter (stuff) in an object. The force of gravity pulls on everything with mass, so the more mass something has, the more it weighs.

MIXTURE

A substance made of two or more compounds or elements. A mixture can be any mixed of solids, liquids, and gases. Air is a mixture of gases.

MOLECULE

Two or more atoms joined together.

ORBIT

The path of a planet, comet, or asteroid around the Sun— or the path of a moon or a satellite around a planet. The force of gravity keeps objects in their orbits.

pH

A measure of the concentration of hydrogen ions in a solution. The more hydrogen ions, the lower the pH and the more acidic the solution.

PIGMENT

A colorful substance. Inks, paints, and flowers all contain pigments.

PRESSURE

A measure of how much a force pushes on a surface.

PYRAMID

A three-dimensional shape with a point at the top and a triangle or a square at the base.

RADIATION

The loss of heat from a hot object (as it gives out infrared radiation). Also about for electromagnetic radiation. Light, infrared, ultraviolet, radio waves, and X-rays are all forms of electromagnetic radiation.

RECYCLING

The process of reusing something that is no longer needed.

SOLUTION

A mixture where one substance is dissolved in a liquid.

SOUND WAVE

An invisible wave that travels through air (or through liquids and solids) as alternating zones of high and low pressure.

SPECTRUM

A spread of colors produced by splitting light into the colors of which it is made, as happens in a rainbow.

TENSION

A pulling force; the opposite of compression.

TURBINE

A device with rotating fan blades that are driven by the pressure of gases, liquids, or steam. Turbines powered by the wind or by moving water are often used to generate electricity.

VIBRATION

A very rapid back-and-forth movement. Guitar strings vibrate when you pluck them, creating sound waves.

VOLUME

The amount of space something takes up, normally measured in milliliters, liters, or cubic meters.

WAVELENGTH

The distance between two peaks of a wave. In a sound wave, the wavelength is the distance between one point of highest air pressure and the next.

WEIGHT

The downward force on an object caused by gravity. The more mass something has, the more it weighs.

INDEX

ACKNOWLEDGMENTS

Smithsonian Enterprises:

Carol LeBlanc, Senior Vice President, Consumer and Education Products;
Brigid Ferraro, Vice President, Consumer and Education Products; Ellen
Nanney, Licensing Manager; Kealy Gordon, Product Development Manager

Curator for the Smithsonian:

Tim Pula, Interpretive Exhibit Coordinator Spark!Lab,
Lemelson Center, National Museum of American History

The publisher would like to thank the following people for their
assistance in the preparation of this book:

Sam Atkinson and Pauline Savage for editorial assistance; Smiljka Surla for
design assistance; Steve Crozier and Adam Brackenbury for picture

retouching; Pankaj Sharma, Ashok Kumar, Nityanand Kumar, and Jagtar
Singh for repro work; Sean T. Ross for testing the experiments; Clarisse
Hassan for additional illustrations; Helen Peters for indexing; Victoria Pyke
for proofreading; Emmie-Mae Avery, Amelia Collins, Lex Hebblethwaite,
Mollie Penfold, Melissa Sinclair, Kelly Wray, Abi Wright for hand modelling.

The publisher would like to thank the following for their kind
permission to reproduce their photographs:
(Key: a-above, b-below/bottom, c-centre, f-far, l-left, r-right, t-top).

17 Dreamstime.com: Masezdromaderi (tr); **Getty Images:** Stringer / Bill
Pugliano / Getty Images News (cr). **23 Getty Images:** Jeff Rotman / The
Image Bank (bl). **29 iStockphoto.com:** BlackJack3D (crb). **37
Dreamstime.com:** Toldiu74 (bl). **41 Alamy Stock Photo:** Michele and Tom
Grimm (crb). **49 Dreamstime.com:** Andrey Shupilo (br). **59 Dreamstime.**

com: Vladislav Kochelaevskiy (br). **65 iStockphoto.com:** oversnap (bl). **69
Depositphotos Inc:** alexlmx (br). **77 Dorling Kindersley:** Stephen Oliver
(crb). **81 Dreamstime.com:** Andrey Armyagov (bl). **93 Dreamstime.com:**
Jarrun Klinmontha (crb). **97 Dorling Kindersley:** Natural History Museum,
London / Harry Taylor (cb); **Dreamstime.com:** Horseman 82 (clb); **Science
Photo Library:** Steve Lowry (crb). **105 123RF.com:** Songquan Deng (crb);
Dreamstime.com: Ian Klein (clb). **111 Science Photo Library:** Laguna
Design (bl). **117 Dreamstime.com:** Hayati Kayhan (br). **123 The Reinforced
Earth Company:** (br). **131 Dreamstime.com:** STRINGERimages (cra). **137
NASA: ESA / Hubble & NASA** (bl). **141 Getty Images:** Inti St Clair /
Blend Images (bl). **145 Dreamstime.com:** Elitsa Lambova (br). **149 Rex by
Shutterstock:** AP (bc). **157 Dreamstime.com:** Mrchan (br).

All other images © Dorling Kindersley.

For further information see: www.dkimages.com